IN HIS OWN WORDS

George Michael

GEORGE MICHAEL..IN HIS OWN WORDS

Exclusive distributors:

Book Sales Limited
8-9 Frith Street, London W1V 5TZ, UK

Music Sales Corporation
257 Park Avenue South, New York, NY 10010, USA

Five Mile Press
22 Summit Road, Noble Park, Victoria 3174, Australia

Exclusive distributors to the music trade only:

Music Sales Limited
8-9 Frith Street, London W1V 5TZ, UK

ISBN 0.7119.7891.3
Order No. OP48160

Copyright © 1999 Omnibus Press
(A Division of Book Sales Limited)

Photo credits: Richard Young/Rex: front cover, 4, 102, 105, 106 t&b, 108 t&b, 110,;
Davies & Starr/Retna: 44; Oken Friedman/Retna: 26b; Gary Gershoff/Retna: 3b,
109;Mick Hutson/Redferns: 31, 33t, 35, 40, 51b, 61t, 91t, 92t, 96t; London Features
International: 3t, 6, 7, 8b, 9t, 9b, 10, 11, 12b, 13, 14, 16, 17t, 18, 19t, 19br, 21, 22b, 23,
24, 27t, 28, 32, 33b, 39b, 41 t&b, 43b, 46b, 47, 48, 49t, 50, 51t, 54, 55, 57, 58, 62, 65t,
66, 67, 76 t&b, 79t, 82, 86, 87 t&b, 89 t&b, 94, 100: Neil Matthews/Retna:17b;
Walter Mcbride/Retna: 22t, 26t, 52; Michael Melia/Retna: 91b; Frank Micelotta/Retna:
96b; Neal Preston/Retna: 43t; Michael Putland/Retna: 15, 19bl, 20, 27b, 30t, 38, 39t, 42,
46t, 60, 64, 68, 69b, 70, 72, 93; Rex Features: back cover, 2, 5, 29, 61b, 69t, 73b, 74,
75, 77, 79b, 80, 81, 83, 84, 85, 88, 90, 92b, 95, 97, 98, 99 101, 103, 104 t&b, 107, 111,
112; S&G/Redferns: 78; Troy/Retna: 12t; Rob Verhorst/Redferns: 30b, 34, 36 t&b, 37, 59,
73t; David Wainwright/Retna: 56; Scott Weiner/Retna:s 8t, 49b.

Edited by Chris Charlesworth

Series design concept by **Michael Bell Design**

Cover and new material originated by **Hilite**

Picture research by David Brolan & Nikki Russell

Every effort has been made to trace the copyright holders of
the photographs in this book but one or two were unreachable.
We would be grateful if the photographers concerned would
contact us.

Printed in Great Britain by Page Bros. Ltd, Norwich, Norfolk.

Visit Omnibus Press at
www.omnibuspress.com

OMNIBUS PRESS

CONTENTS

Introduction

In 1990 George Michael, tired of banal questions about his personal life, decided not to give any more interviews in the foreseeable future, thus making a collection of his quotes a challenge to compile but fascinating to read. Nevertheless, following his much-publicised indiscretion in a public Park in Los Angeles and subsequent decision to 'come out' as a gay man, he has been more talkative than ever before.

Michael's career began in the early Eighties when he formed the pop duo Wham! with his longtime friend Andrew Ridgeley. They were two bronzed wideboys who looked like they had escaped from a Club 18-30 Holiday. The media thought Wham! and George Michael would last all of 15 minutes. They could not have been more wrong. They became international teen idols thanks to their catchy songs and undeniable sex appeal. After Wham! George Michael shed his teenybopper image and changed from plump, pimply bouffant-boy to a lean, mean, designer stubble hit machine and emerged as a serious composer, singer and producer whose talents have evoked comparisons with Paul McCartney and Elton John.

Up to the time he clammed up, George rarely shied away from talking to the media, and most of the quotes in this book come from the late Eighties when he spoke freely. Quotes from immediately after his self-imposed "no talking" ban come from transcriptions of the court proceedings between George and Sony Music which took place in October 1993, and a lengthy TV interview he gave to David Frost after judgement went against him. During 1998 George opened up again, perhaps relieved that the veil of secrecy surrounding his personal life had been lifted.

Nigel Goodall, June 1999

With special thanks to Keith Hayward and Kate King for their invaluable assistance. And to Pamela Craddock at *Q* Magazine.

Early Days

My name is Georgios Kyriacos Panayiotou. To the outside world I am, and always will be, known as something else. But it's not my name. As a boy my biggest fear was that my huge ambitions would stay just out of reach of the child I saw in the mirror. So I created a man that the world could love if they chose to, someone who could realise my dreams and make me a star. I called him George Michael, and for almost a decade he worked non-stop for me and did as he was told. He was very good at his job, perhaps a little too good. Anyway, shortly before I wrote all this down, I decided that his services were no longer required. I know many of you will think that it was a strange thing for me to do, but believe me, he really had to go ...
Press Statement 1993

That was what I wanted to be right from being a child, but I had no idea I could sing and no idea I could play. I had a go at the violin as a kid – I was bloody awful and hated doing it, then I played the drums, briefly, at the age of 12. I didn't know how I was going to do it, but I had this feeling that I was definitely going to be in showbusiness as a pop star.
Daily Express 1990

I definitely wanted attention. At school I needed a group of followers, but I got a real lousy group.
Daily Express 1990

George's first band, The Executive: George and Andrew Ridgeley (seated) with David Mortimer and Andrew Leaver.

When I was about nine, I realised that I dominated the people I went around with. Suddenly I realised that I didn't want to. I felt slightly unpleasant doing it. I completely changed and I remember thinking I'm not going to boss people about. Then I moved schools and met Andrew (Ridgeley). He was the first friend I had that was as strong as me characterwise, and that's why I didn't really need any others after that.

Daily Express 1990

I actually went to school in North London and then my secondary education between the ages of twelve and seventeen was in Hertfordshire.

Chancery High Court 1993

I don't think I was particularly educated at seventeen or eighteen. I did English literature and art.

Chancery High Court 1993

(Above): George's parents, Jack and Lesley Panayiotou.

After I refused to go to a private school – which would have killed my parents financially – my dad gave up on me career-wise. I didn't want to go to a private school because my friends would have called me a sissy. Plus I would have been intimidated by it and I really didn't want to be with those kind of people. Lots of reasons!
Bare 1990

I remember my first bet. My father gave me a fiver, I put it on a horse and the thing came in at 8-1.
Sunday Express 1994

I am so different now – just through losing some weight and growing my hair and doing different things. I looked a hell of a lot worse as a kid.
Daily Express 1990

I was a cinema usher and a builder's labourer. I had a Saturday job at British Home Stores but got the sack for not wearing a shirt and tie in the stock room.
The Sun 1990

I was fat and ugly and I had glasses. I also had one big bushy eyebrow. I have now had it treated to make two eyebrows. For years I would try and grow my hair long to cover it.
Daily Express 1990

I had a very mobile childhood, both in terms of moving from the city to the suburbs and of moving from working class to middle class. I can't think of a more stable situation for me to have grown up in because I didn't really experience any of the hard times at the beginning.
Daily Mail 1990

The first sign of my obsession with music was with an old wind-up gramophone that Mum had thrown out into the garage. My parents gave me three old 45s, two Supremes records and one Tom Jones record, and I used to come home from school every day, go out to the garage, wind this thing up and play them.
Daily Mail 1990

I was totally obsessed with the idea of the records; I loved them as things, and just being able to listen to music was incredible. Later they (my parents) bought me a cassette with a microphone that I used to tape things from the radio – and then I became even more obsessive.
Daily Mail 1990

When I first went to school and until the age of about nine or ten,
I was just above average height, quite a cute little kid, very popular.
No insecurity there. But then, just at the age when your hormones
are popping up and everything is changing, my dad decided to move
house and we moved to this big place in Radlett, which is in
Hertfordshire. It was a real old hole and it took a year to decorate.
Daily Mail 1990

It was okay for Andrew (Ridgeley) to be on the dole because
he was still living at home and he was a lazy bastard who just didn't
want to go out to work. I worked on a building site, I was a DJ in
a restaurant, I was a cinema usher.
Daily Mail 1990

I hadn't known it at the time, but the turning point in my early
days was meeting Andrew Ridgeley at secondary school. He'd looked
good, got the girls and wanted to be famous. He changed my life.
Daily Mail 1990

Eventually I realised that I was used to a lifetime of putting
myself down physically. The strongest years of your life when it
comes to thinking about your looks are between 12 and 15, and
because I looked pretty naff then it was almost as if I had a complex
about it. I felt faintly ridiculous being screamed at.
Daily Express 1990

My parents used to let me bring home anyone I liked – but they didn't like Andrew (Ridgeley) at all. He was much more confident than they were used to my friends being, he didn't have any of the inhibitions or cautions that most people feel when they walk into someone else's home.
Bare 1990

I remember when Andrew and I were kids he took acid and had the most awful, awful time. A really bad trip. He never took it again for years and years and years. Just his description of what happened to him really put me off. Anyway, I'm just too much of a control freak and really couldn't handle the idea of things coming at me and not being able to stop it. I still hear horrible stories about things happening to people on stuff like acid. It's just too extreme for me.
Q 1990

My parents were rock and roll dancers. They met at a dance and my father used to throw my mother all over the show. There are some really cool pictures of my dad which they never used to show me when I was growing up because they were afraid that I could point to them and say – well, look, you did it.
Bare 1990

I used to babysit over the road from our house and Andrew (Ridgeley) would come over. We would put on 'Stuff Like That' by Quincey Jones and make up a little dance routine where we would walk rather stupidly across the room. Not one of our best.
Bare 1990

There were things going on when I was growing up that I never understood. Things that make me really admire my mum. If there's anything I've got from her, it's that she's like a rock. I've got that stability from her.
Sunday Times 1993

I was a terrible dancer but Andrew (Ridgeley) and I worked out these routines that we could do at school discos. That would have been when I was fourteen – I had just got my first contact lenses.
Bare 1990

We (George and childhood friend David Mortimer) used to do David Bowie numbers and some Elton John songs. We had written a few things and we did those too. And Beatles things. I loved it, I loved busking. I loved the way it sounded – the way the voice and guitar would reverberate down the tube station. And I loved it that we were good and that we were getting paid for it.
Bare 1990

Before *Saturday Night Fever* I was blind to that kind of music. You didn't hear a lot of dance on the radio, everybody was still into the 1960s and early 1970s idea of getting into your own thing at home. *Saturday Night Fever* got me out to the clubs. By the time I was fifteen I was even busking so that I had the money to go to the clubs.
Bare 1990

Me and my dad were having this big argument. We were driving in the car and I was playing him this demo tape. Apart from 'Rude Boy' I had done something with David (Mortimer) and I was plugging this thing around all the record companies as well. And I remember playing it in the car to my dad and he was going on about how I had to realise that there was no future in this for me. He had been telling me all this for years and I had given up arguing with him long ago – I knew he wouldn't take any notice. But now I really had a go at him. I said, "You have been rubbing this shit into my face for the last five years". I told him, "There is no way I am not going to try to do this, so the least you could do is give me some moral support."
Bare 1990

One of the most incredible moments of my life was hearing 'Careless Whisper' demo'ed properly, with a band and a sax and everything. It was ironic that we signed the contract with Mark (Dean) that day, the day I finally believed that we had number one material. The same day we signed it all away. But you can never really know what you are capable of, you can never really have that foresight.
Bare 1990

I had been trying to get a deal with either a publisher or a record company for roughly two years. I went to many record companies, but the only ones I remember are the major ones. I went to Chrysalis, A&M, EMI, Virgin. I don't actually recall all the names of the various companies I went to. Basically the A&R departments showed no interest and I played tapes of demos and they weren't interested.
Chancery High Court 1993

We had a £20 demo tape that we had recorded in Andrew's front room. What we wanted was for someone to give us £200 to do it in a studio. We were just looking for a chance to prove the songs 'Careless Whisper', 'Wham Rap', 'Club Tropicana' and 'Come On'. We went to music publishers at Virgin and about half a dozen other places and we used to turn up and pretend we had appointments.

Otherwise they would never have agreed to see us. We had a
little routine – we would first be nice and then pretend that the
secretary had made a mistake and get very angry... it really did work.
We got into most of the big publishers that way, just turned up and
did our routine. They nearly always believed you. They normally
listened to the tape in our presence. Usually, they would turn it
off after about ten or fifteen seconds. They used to tell us it was
rubbish and send us away.
Daily Mail 1990

I had nearly made my stage début with The Quiffs. They were
some of the people Andrew knew from college; he was probably
smoking dope with these guys. And one night their drummer
dropped out. I could play the drums and they knew I could, but they
took one look at me and said I couldn't do it. I didn't look the part –
I just looked too bad. I remember being crushed by that.
Daily Mail 1990

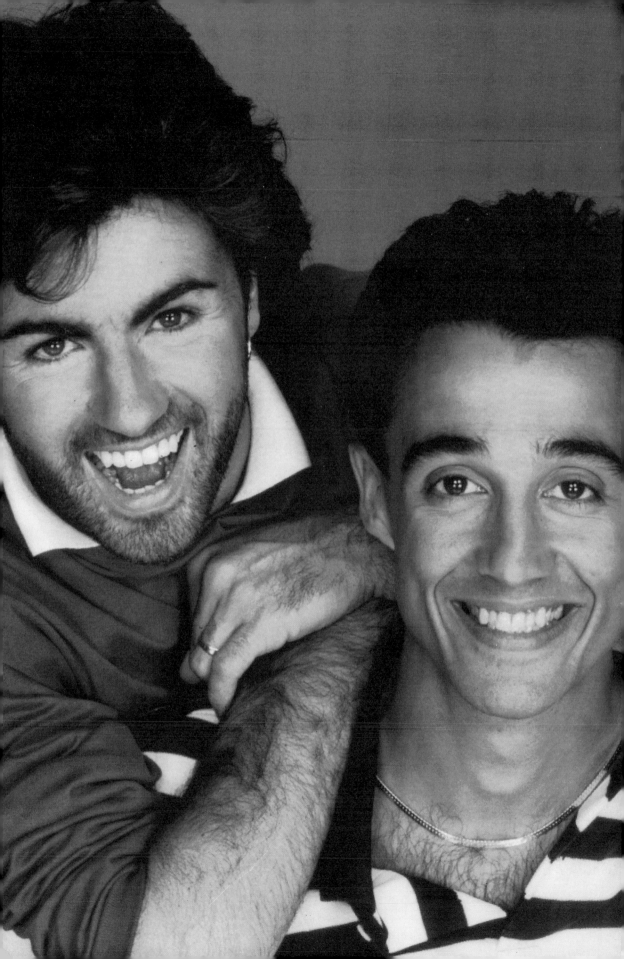

Wham!

There was a period of about two or three months when Andrew (Ridgeley) and I first came to London to meet the people from CBS and I thought – now I'm here and someone will show me what to do. A publishing company wants my songs. The label wants to turn the songs into records. And here I am. Someone, I thought, would let me in on the secret, expose me to the machinery, show me how it turns two kids with some songs into pop stars. And then after two months it clicked – the machinery doesn't exist. The record industry is a bunch of headless chickens, no one knows anything. They couldn't tell me what to do because they didn't know themselves. After I realised that it was easy. Because then I knew I had to do it all myself.
Bare 1990

When Andrew and I started Wham! we had a very strong gay following and I still have it. I don't bother denying it anymore. I know what I am and so do my friends. That's all that matters today.
Today 1990

Andrew said he wanted us to be the biggest group in the world. I think he just saw that I had to be let off the reins.
Today 1990

Our very first PA was at a club called Level One in Neasden. And it was terrible because there were six hundred people in this club and, because there was no raised stage, they just formed a big circle around us. And so you are doing this thing and you have two really attractive girls with you, and you are trying to play out this little scenario between two couples – just like on *Top Of The Pops* – but you had all the drunks coming up and joining in! And the drunks would go up behind the girls. It was an absolute nightmare.
Bare 1990

We did Stringfellow's, I remember that was a really embarrassing one. There was a kick in the first routine. I did this kick and my shoe flew off into the crowd – so then I kicked the other one off with great aplomb to make it look deliberate. And I had to keep going. I was dancing in socks on the glass floor of Stringfellow's and trying desperately not to cock it up, trying not to fall flat on my face. I was holding the fake mike with the fake lead and I remember going to the side of the dance floor with this thing and I felt the lead pull out, which totally exposed me as miming to the track.
Bare 1990

Some people just thought we were prats. They thought that bloke poncing around in the pretty blond hair with the shorts and the teeth was me. They couldn't understand that it was me trying to be the ultimate performer. In fact, we were the first group since the days of The Beatles who didn't relate their personalities to their music.
1986

I said I wanted to release 'Careless Whisper' and people said it was bad timing. They said "No, don't do it. Wham! is just taking off. You'll confuse people". But I know 'Careless Whisper' was my strongest song and that it would go to No.1 – and it did.
Daily Express 1990

I reached a dilemma when Wham! decided that they were going to Ibiza to make videos and get brown. I decided that I wanted to write songs without any restraints.
Today 1990

George and Andrew with Shirlie Holliman and Pepsi De Manque.

Without Andrew, I couldn't have kept up the bright young thing image. It wasn't me, it was him. His personality was greater than mine.

1986

Being seen as an attractive person during the Wham! time was very exciting for me because I was only 18 or 19. I was thrilled to be suddenly looked upon as a physically attractive human being.

Daily Express 1988

We were out and out pop. We thought it was the most honest thing to do. We didn't want to be subversive in any sense. We wanted to be huge stars. I knew that I could do it. I knew that I had the capability, craftwise, to put us ahead of groups like Duran Duran and Culture Club, so I just went for it.

The Times 1990

I was deliberately appealing to young girls in a kind of non-sexual way. It was deliberately feminine in the sense that that's what young girls want at a certain age – nothing that looks vaguely hairy or threatening. A lot of pop groups were like that – look at Duran Duran or Boy George.

The Times 1990

I began to feel uncomfortable with the cleanliness of it. Wham! was a concept we had when we were young, when we didn't know anything about anything. Andrew was still completely into the lifestyle, but I was growing up a bit.

The Times 1990

Wham! as flight crew,
with Shirlie Holliman and D. C. Lee.

As Wham!, Andrew and I had gone from being unknowns to household names – even a fraught legal battle with our first record company hadn't stopped the string of hits. But soon I was doing most of the work while Andrew was out getting wrecked. The imbalance began to tell.
Daily Mail 1990

Andrew was really starting to feel my songwriting ambitions begin to accelerate. I wasn't trying to edge him out or anything but it was just so obvious that was where it was going in terms of writing. And it is only because we didn't talk about it that it became a tense subject. But once we talked about it we got out of the way and we never talked about it again. We never needed to.
Bare 1990

Andrew and I couldn't have run about in shorts and done the 'Club Tropicana' video if we had been the colour of dead goldfishes. Because there was something vaguely Mediterranean about us we were totally convincing when we went the 'Club Tropicana' route where two boys who were completely English wouldn't have been. I think that was part of the attraction.
Bare 1990

We thought that if they were going to write rubbish about us, we might as well know what kind of rubbish it was. So we made most of it up and we had quite a laugh until we realised that we were making fools of ourselves by letting them print it all.
Wham! Confidential 1987

One month I'd be fat, fascist, homosexual, with a huge
Georgian house somewhere in Essex. The next I'd be a lean, virile
Left winger.
Wham! Confidential 1987

The final appearance of Wham! at Wembley was incredible,
but strangely it was so important to me that it didn't register
immediately. I don't think I enjoyed it enough, but watching the
videos now is absolutely stunning. I have never seen a crowd like
that – for anyone at any concert, apart perhaps for Live Aid.
In retrospect, I know that it was really perfect. The weather was
perfect, the people were perfect and the band was great. Everything
in the whole series of Wham! events seemed so blessed that it was
just the cherry on the cake.
Daily Mail 1990

No way could I have done it without Andrew. I can't think of
anybody I have ever met in my life who would have been so perfect
in allowing something, which started out as a very naïve, joint
ambition, to become what was still a huge double act but was
really... mine. I have never met anyone who would be strong or
generous enough to let that happen. He contributed so much.
It was one of those things that just makes you think it was all meant
to happen. The luckiest thing that ever happened to me was meeting
Andrew, he totally shaped my life. Not just those years but the
whole thing – he totally shaped it and I would never begrudge him
that credit. People put him down... you don't defend someone at
the dinner table by mentioning that they totally shaped your life.
But that's the way I feel about him.
Bare 1990

Going Solo

At the end of Wham! I needed a new challenge. So I set
myself the challenge of getting up there on the American level with
Madonna and Jackson – that circle of people. That was my goal.
And then having got into that position I realised that it wasn't really
my... it wasn't really going to do anything for me. I can honestly say
most of 1988 was a complete nightmare for me.
Sunday Correspondent 1990

After Wham! split everyone expected better things from me.
But I don't regret the break-up. I had prepared myself for the fact
that Wham! was going to end. For the last couple of years, Wham!
was very much my venture, anyway, so it wasn't so frightening.
The pressure is on Andrew (Ridgeley) now. He is working on an
album and I've advised him. It's only natural that the public is going
to be sceptical about his work. He's going to surprise them, though,
because his music is a lot better than people think.
Today 1987

My personal ambition now is to become more successful worldwide.
I want to reach the same level I'm on in Britain everywhere,
especially America.
Today 1987

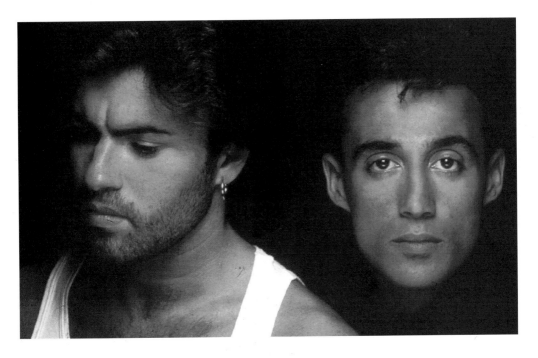

I don't think my going solo has been any better or worse. It's just been different. Most people watch a split like Wham! split and wait for a fall, but I am extremely pleased with the direction of my career. Music is a passion that keeps me going 24 hours a day.
Today 1987

After my years with Wham! I felt I had to go out and prove I could have a successful album by myself. The next album will probably be softer, more relaxed and acoustic and probably not as aggressively commercial.
1989

When I decided to split with Andrew (Ridgeley) I was in the middle of a very heavy depression. I had personal problems at the time. I was going through the end of a relationship and I was feeling very negative about the whole Wham! thing. I was feeling trapped by a lot of things.
Daily Mail 1990

Perhaps my darkest days came after the break up of Wham! I got heavily into booze, but I was doing a fair bit of drugs as well. I wasn't taking coke. Still to this day, I don't take coke. For a while I took Ecstasy when it was not very available over here. I took it simply because it made me feel that everything was wonderful. It wasn't, of course.
Daily Mail 1990

I woke up one morning, and I realised that there had been a period in Wham! when I had actually completely forgotten who I was. I had this depression for about eight months. It was a very self-pitying thing, sense of isolation and all that stuff. I started losing my temper for the first time in my life too. I suddenly realised I have a vicious temper. I got into fist fights with friends, threw photographers against walls, acted very macho... terrible. In that period I lost my temper six or eight times. I wasn't drunk because there was no excuse for my behaviour, the people that knew me who saw it were horrified. I'd go completely out of character. My voice would drop about an octave and I'd start talking with this incredibly heavy slang. A lot of it was not having a person there to say to me, Look, what the fuck have you of all people got to complain about? A combination of things set it off. Wham! split up and I came out of a bad relationship. For a time I thought I really didn't want to get back into the music business when we finished Wham! The problem was just that I had developed a character for the outside world that wasn't me, and I was having to deal with people all the time who thought it was.

So I made the decision to uncreate the person I had created and become more real. In retrospect I don't think I could have made as clean a transition between Wham! and me without it. I needed a period where I could put things into perspective. One night during this depression I went out to see Andrew in LA and got pissed out of my head and poured it all out, and until that moment, the way I felt and what I was really thinking hadn't crystallised. When I heard it actually come out of my own mouth it was like an exorcism. I saw him again last week when he came out to Hawaii. He worries about me being at the centre of all this fuss again without anyone to bounce off. We talked and I reassured him that I can cope with it all a lot better than I could before.
Q 1988

Wham! were dead, but my problems hadn't disappeared with the band's demise. Andrew and I were still good friends, but broken relationships, a bout of heavy boozing and a fair bit of drugs hadn't made my life any easier. Somewhere along the line I had to make a radical change.
Daily Mail 1990

The Records

I was really happy being a singles artist, the whole medium
excited me, because it was so short term and you could see an
immediate result. These days I just don't have the same objectives.
Bare 1990

I think I have a record number of plays at Radio One on two
or three of my records, and that is principally down to, I would like
to think, the quality of the records and the relationship with my
audience.
Chancery High Court 1993

I'll always make records because I love music. But I don't enjoy
being in the business. I don't enjoy the hardening process that has
already begun. I look at people who have been in the music business
a long time and I know I don't want to be like them.
Daily Mail 1990

I have had four albums really in my career and I actually think
that each of them has been quite different from the album before,
but they have all stayed within the mainstream. I think my music
has changed quite drastically, but I would say that the consistency
in it would be that it is mainstream.
Chancery High Court 1993

My reviews have never had any effect on my sales.
Chancery High Court 1993

I do make a real point of looking to see where my new material is
advertised, where it's placed in stores, that kind of thing. I do make
a real point of going in and looking.
Chancery High Court 1993

Cassette singles earlier in my career were not important.
The cassette single has risen in the USA within the last two, three,
four years, very much so, but I have always been of the impression
that the Top Ten records in America are very much sparred for by
record companies by way of promotion within the stores and
reduction in cost.
Chancery High Court 1993

The way the American chart appears to work is that singles move purely, or almost entirely, on radio airplay to a certain degree, and they move at a natural rate, which for me is normally that they come in reasonably high and move fairly quickly. And then when you get to the Top 15, Top 10, what really starts to go is a radio and retail sparring between record companies where they fight for position, and what was happening was that my records were going in at their normal reasonably high positions, moving quickly, and then at that stage stopping or slowing down considerably, and I gained the very strong impression that what was happening then was that the record company was not basically making that last effort or actually putting the money into basically what creates a Top Five or Top Three single.
Chancery High Court 1993

If an album is exploited in the industry today it is exploited fully. You're talking about making the videos, doing the tours. Really if you were to complete an album and then promote and exploit it for a year that would be your two-year period, and in reality it doesn't really leave you any time to live... to have a life to write about in all honesty. You don't really want to write about touring and promoting your last album. So ultimately I think that's probably why people who get to a certain level in the industry now take on average about three years between albums simply because the actual process of recording and writing, and then the process of exploiting, takes roughly a two year chunk out of your life. So I think three years is a fairly common distance between albums now.
Chancery High Court 1993

B-sides are normally seen as some kind of second rate piece of material, but certain other artists that I have noticed in the last four or five years have been really making a feature, especially to an adult audience, of new material for B-sides. If someone already has an album and they have the track that you're releasing as a single on the album, there's an incentive for them to buy the single even though they already have the album if they have a new B side. But to do that, to actually make people aware of that change – because historically I had instrumentals or tracks that had already been released or other tracks from the album on B-sides. And to make people aware that something different was going on and that there was a reason to buy the single, I felt it was necessary to have a major print advertising, as other bands had, and that was the campaign I was really talking about not happening. So after, I think, the first two singles from 'Listen Without Prejudice' I actually stopped concentrating on making B-sides because they weren't exploited in any way.
Chancery High Court 1993

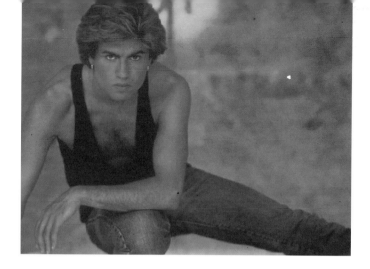

Wake Me Up Before You Go Go

I think 'Go Go' is undoubtedly the most remembered Wham! song because it is that much more stupid than anything else! I still look at that video and think it worked really perfectly for that song. Really poppy, really colourful – it totally captures that whole period. But although I see it working as a video, it makes me cringe for myself. But I was completely into the idea of being screamed at – I was very young and I can't pretend my ego didn't need that.
Daily Mail 1990

Careless Whisper

The very last night I worked as a DJ I played the demo of 'Careless Whisper'. I knew it didn't matter if I got into trouble because I had already given in my notice the week before.
So right at the end of the night, I played it and... the floor filled. They had never heard it before and the floor filled. I remember thinking, "That's a good sign". And I wondered what was going to happen to that song.
Daily Mail 1990

We knocked off Duran Duran from number one, then Frankie Goes To Hollywood knocked us off, then 'Careless Whisper' knocked them off. I really loved all that. I never felt threatened. I must admit I never thought the Frankies would be around for very long. All the English bands were dependent on other people for songwriting, production, you name it.
Bare 1990

'Careless Whisper' was not an integral part of my emotional development. It's sad because that song means so much to so many people. It disappoints me that you can write a lyric very flippantly – and not a particularly good lyric – and it can mean so much to so many people. That's disillusioning for a writer.
Bare 1990

Do They Know It's Christmas

I felt very uncomfortable in the studio when we did the Band Aid thing. I was very aware of the prejudice against Wham! in there. Everybody in there had said things about everyone else in the press and, to a lot of people, Wham! were the laughing stock of the year. Some of it was jealousy and some of it was a genuine lack of respect. But the only person who actually came up and had a go at me was Paul Weller because of something I had said about Arthur Scargill, the leader of the miners. I just said what I believed – I think the man's a wanker. Wham! did that benefit for the families of the miners, not for Scargill.

Bare 1990

Different Corner

I had to write something. I had to get it out and I did it in a couple of days. It was the first time I used my own experience and emotions for a song. The pain comes back when I perform or hear it. At first I couldn't even listen to it, especially when I was trying to get over the emotions I was singing about.

Daily Mail 1990

I Want Your Sex

Once free of the Wham! connection, my first solo single got me into real trouble. 'I Want Your Sex' was condemned by many and banned by a few. Not surprisingly, then, it was a success. But I still feel outraged by the reaction of a lot of people to that record.

Daily Mail 1990

I wanted to reach a new bunch of fans with 'I Want Your Sex', and it worked well in the States. But I couldn't attract new fans in Britain – because of the IBA ban, nobody heard it.

Today 1987

American Rap music and Heavy Metal are so aggressively sexual in a completely distasteful way – and I didn't think 'I Want Your Sex' was at all. I like the idea of it being aggressively sexual, but you had to get the idea that the aggression was the lust. The only way I was going to get the sex was with consent. It wasn't about trying to make someone do something – it was trying to show how much you wanted them. I wasn't at all comfortable with being a sex spokesman – I didn't see why anyone should ask me. The song anyway wasn't

just about fucking – it was about fucking within a relationship.
It was the time of the first big Aids scare over here and they were on
the second wave over in America and it really pissed me off the way
the issue was being treated. All these scare tactics – tell your kids that
sex is something they shouldn't do, at least until we find a cure for
this thing. Which is such a lot of bollocks – and you can't take the
sex out of the music industry because that's what it's built on.
My whole point was that there should be an attack on promiscuity
but you could do it without making kids frightened of sex.
Bare 1990

When I released 'I Want Your Sex', and the music video, I didn't
think the image would have such a lasting effect. The image still
seems to overshadow the music.
1989

George with Kathy Jeuing
during the making of the video
for 'I Want Your Sex'.

Faith

My single 'Faith' was inspired by a couple of relationships that
didn't happen. Very soon after the break-up of the group and before
I started seeing Kathy, there were people with whom I thought
about starting relationships – and eventually decided against it.
Because I knew I was on the rebound and I wanted to be with
someone for a different reason than that.
Daily Mail 1990

To me the album was about an affirmation of faith – because
before that period of my life there had been a lack of it. As I said,
coming out of the Wham! thing I felt as if some big joke had
been played on me. I had led myself to believe I had everything –
I dreamed of realising certain aspirations and they had all happened
but I still felt there was a big gap, a massive hole in my life that
I was never going to be able to fill. That was the way I felt at the
end of Wham! What 'Faith' meant – the album, the campaign, all
of it – was that I had faith life was going to deliver, that I was going
to get the things I wanted, that my life would bring me the things
that are important to me.
Bare 1990

The 'Faith' album had been extremely successful in America
on the Black charts. I think I was the first artist to actually have a

number one single on the Black charts who wasn't actually black, and after that I received two major awards at the American Music Awards, which were historically Black awards, and that created quite a lot of controversy, and I think quite rightly so.
Chancery High Court 1993

I can assure you that it was far, far easier to see in-store advertising for 'Faith' than it was for 'Listen Without Prejudice', unless somehow I was deluding myself that there was a lot more advertising for 'Faith'.
Chancery High Court 1993

With 'Faith' I didn't tour in the States until the autumn of 1988, by which time we'd sold almost six million copies of 'Faith', and I don't think that the potential for a tour or cancelling a very small tour had any real effect on the sales of the album.
Chancery High Court 1993

Listen Without Prejudice

With other albums I have been exhausted and by the end, glad they were over. With this one, I felt like carrying on and on.
The Mirror 1990

It was a slightly more adult album, but I didn't feel that 'Faith' was a very young album, I felt that 'Faith' captured a middle ground, and also remembering that most of the people who bought 'Faith' would be three years older. I don't think that the market I was appealing to was particularly different. I think that the market that I had attracted in 'Faith', in the United States maybe more than in other territories, a lot of that market was attracted on a visual basis. But musically I didn't think there was a huge, huge disparity between the two albums.
Chancery High Court 1993

I think Michael Jackson's sales for a start were so phenomenal on 'Thriller' that you wouldn't expect to follow them up with the same thing. I think that was a phenomenon which was far outside of most projections for an album. But I don't actually accept the point that 'Listen Without Prejudice' was bound to be substantially... in terms of the quality of the album I don't accept that it was destined to do far, far worse, and I'm afraid I think that the UK performance backs that feeling up.
Chancery High Court 1993

Red Hot & Dance

It was actually a re-mix album. I'd been approached by, I don't
know, maybe a couple of months before that, maybe not quite so
long, and I was going to give them a track from 'Listen Without
Prejudice' to re-mix and then later on, when I decided that I was
not going to make a dance album or even half a dance album,
I decided almost immediately after that to give those three tracks
that I was considering, or three of the four tracks I was considering
for 'Listen Without Prejudice Volume II', to 'Red Hot & Dance',
almost immediately afterwards.
Chancery High Court 1993

I think its importance was, firstly, as a charity album, and secondly
as an album which had three brand new compositions and recordings
of mine on it, and therefore should have been of some importance
I would have thought to Sony worldwide, simply because it included
new material from one of their artists.
Chancery High Court 1993

The many people around the world who will benefit from the 'Red
Hot & Dance' project need all the support we can give them. It is
a shame this fact was overlooked. This lack of support was apparent
in the chart show's refusal to play the 'Too Funky' video. It seems
this negative approach has more to do with people's perception of
George Michael than anything else.
The Mirror 1992

**George with the 'Too Funky'
video supermodels.**

I would say that if you spend nothing in marketing you're going to have very little to hand over. If you spend some in marketing then hopefully you've produced a result that will enable you to hand over a lot of money to the charity. Also I was aware of the fact that most of the advertising I was seeing in the press was donated very kindly by those publications to the charity.

Chancery High Court 1993

Don't Let The Sun Go Down On Me (Duet with Elton John)

It's a tragic coincidence that our record should be out now. The only good thing is that both our record and the Queen record will help Aids charities.

Too Funky

It did quite well to a point. As with other releases of mine, it moved very, very quickly, due to considerable airplay, and then just outside the Top Ten it stopped.

Chancery High Court 1993

Mothers Pride

'Mothers Pride' was an anti-war song, which could now easily be misinterpreted as a pure cash-in. I had never intended it to be a single. I think many artists would object... and most artists would be respected by their record companies.

Daily Mirror 1993

Songwriting & Performing

My future ambitions lie in writing songs rather than performing them. I consider myself a performer and a songwriter. That is my talent. That is the reason we have been successful. All the other stuff that goes with being a pop star doesn't interest me.
1986

In terms of the peak of the average artist, I reckon I've got another three or four years to go. There will be a point when I say, well , I can't actually go any further than this and then I'll start looking in other directions.
Today 1987

There will come a day when what I am doing is no longer what the public want. I hope I'll see it coming. I think there will be a point where I can't match what I have done before. It happens to just about every artist and the way I am dealing with it is that I hope, because I started so young, that when the time comes there will be other avenues. I want it to happen gracefully because I see so many people fall and it's terrifying for somebody in my position.
Today 1987

Even though I've got a big following, you always need to bring in new fans. I always write different types of records to attract new people and that's how my following is built.
Today 1987

My loyal fans have been with me since my Wham! days and they are now 17 or 18. Obviously, younger kids – around 12 or 13 don't want to listen to the same artists as their older brothers and sisters, so you lose that following. My fans now are very rarely young, they've grown up a bit. I admit I'm flattered by adult attention.
Today 1987

I hate being on the road. I'm constantly on show, I know that every major artist has to do a world tour once in his life. But I know by the time I finish this in November I will feel like I never want to do it again.
Daily Mail 1988

I wouldn't deny that there are certain parts when the bass is synth and sometimes the drums are machines. I don't consider that to be

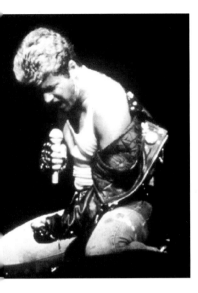

bad. It's all part of the show. All the vocals are me apart from the backing ones. I don't really think it matters that much anyway. I don't think people come to hear a band playing live interpretations of songs any more. This isn't rock'n'roll. I don't play rock'n'roll.
News World 1988

I expected to be dealing with a completely different audience on this tour. I expected a lot less screaming and I didn't really get what I wanted, so maybe I'm over compensating in the raunch department to make up for it. I don't find it shocking though. If I was a guy watching the show I'd think it was funny. If I was watching someone being that cocky up on stage, I'd think it was fun. It's what made Mick Jagger watchable, it's what makes Prince watchable – even Morrissey does it in his own way. I don't expect the critics to disassociate that performer from me as a person because they don't, they just think, fucking big-headed wanker. But it's difficult for me to think of those repercussions when the audience are obviously getting off on it so much. I think it's really funny at the end of the show – it's such a pathetically harmless thing to do – when I put my back to the audience and I take my jacket off really slowly and the place goes absolutely mental. It's just so funny! It's really funny.

But it's not just the girls, if you look at the guys during that bit they're going "Yeah! Go On!" But it's a real dichotomy for me. Because it's impossible to equate the bloke who's doing that with the bloke in the next number, who sings his heart out in a ballad and really means it. People aren't prepared to accept that those two sides exist. I think that's why people are so cynical about me. It's a fortunate position to be in; to be 24 years old and be presentable while still being able to write for a much older age group as well. The two things have just fought each other all the way.
Q 1988

People have always thought my career has been incredibly calculated and premeditated but it runs along pretty well parallel lines with most people's careers, it's just that the decisions I have made personally have been that much more ... correct.
Q 1988

I think people, musicians especially, are jealous. I think mostly people are jealous in that it's all gone too well. Too smoothly. No fuck ups. I often think if there was one major, obvious chink in the armour that people could see, it would be easier for me. People consider what I've done to be too inhuman. The most unfortunate part of that is that I think I've written and sung some of the most human songs I've heard on the radio in the last couple of years. But when you do all the other stuff as neatly as I've done it, it can actually detract from the human element of the songs.
Q 1988

I resent the fact that people think my songwriting is completely contrived and calculated. I only write in terms of commercial music because that's the way my mind works. You either have that sort of pop sensibility or feel for a commercial melody or you don't. You can't write songs on a business level. You just write songs the way they come out. Sure you draw on influences but that's more often than not, a subconscious process. Everybody does it. It's inevitable and I grew up listening to a real mish-mash of music so, of course, the feel of some songs or the drum patterns or whatever, might sound familiar. It would be strange if they didn't.
Q 1988

The audience wants me to be friendly and sexy, and part of me responds to that. But another part of me just wants to play the songs and have the music heard. It goes along with the contradiction between my image and my music.
1989

In a lot of ways I feel that I've just, finally, got rid of a lot of excess baggage. I've got a real feeling of growth now. Although I'm really proud of this album and I feel it really represents me, I have this completely secure feeling inside me that the next one will be much better. I've really learned to relax when I'm making music now. The pressure's off me. I don't have to worry about getting to Number 1, I can just concentrate and enjoy the music. At the moment I'm not in competition with anybody because I have different objectives. In a way I wish that there was someone in the same area that I'm in now so I'd have a sparring partner. But I don't really feel threatened by anyone. In the first part of my career I was threatened by all the other big pop bands like the Frankies and Duran and in the last period it was Madonna and Jackson and Prince. Now that I've made a transition in my head and have moved away from that territory I don't know who there is to compete with.
Q 1990

I get really embarrassed at a party or a dinner if someone asks me to sing. I can't stand it. And my most embarrassing moments as a performer were those first rehearsals at *Top Of The Pops* when there were only eight technicians there. Doing it in front of just a few people always freaked me out.
Bare 1990

We were very aware of how the music business was changing, how you could suddenly reach more people with a video on MTV

than with a ninety-date tour of the States.
Bare 1990

The reason I went to China was because I believed it would be
fascinating, but mainly it was the thought of being the first, it was
an ego satisfaction thing, the idea of being the first to take that sort
of music there. I thought it was something that you just couldn't
turn down. I didn't think of it in terms of making us a bigger band
because we were already big in Britain and Europe, and America had
just taken off. So I wasn't thinking of it in those terms. I'm very glad
we did, it was a great thing to do – but ultimately it was propaganda
for the Chinese Government and publicity for us, nothing more.
Bare 1990

The Live Aid thing was fantastic because the emotion behind it
was genuine – at least on the English side of things. There was lots
of talk about the squabbles that were going on over in Philadelphia
but over here the British bands were too nervous to push themselves
up front, they didn't argue over their spots and it went really well.
Bare 1990

I simply didn't want to conform and make a video like everybody
else. I don't intend to make any videos again. I simply want people
to listen to my music and not look at me. What did people do
15 years ago before videos? They still bought records.
Daily Mirror 1990

When I started out at sixteen, seventeen, I thought of myself as a
songwriter and then my career turned into something that I didn't
expect. After 'Careless Whisper' had been written, I said to Andrew
(Ridgeley) – somebody, somewhere, is going to want to make
money out of these songs. I wasn't convinced that it would be me
who would sing them because I wasn't confident as a singer or
performer and, anyway, I didn't feel that's what my vocation was.
Bare 1990

You can't become an innovator. You are or you aren't. I'm not.
That's why I have to concentrate on being a songwriter.
Q 1990

It ('Freedom') is a very artistic video, and there was nothing
explicit about it. I am extremely disappointed it has been censored
in this way.
The Sun 1990

People aren't naïve now in the way they used to be. I think
music can still influence the way children think. Something like

the acid house movement became a big part of culture but generally individuals don't change things any more. Music wise in this country, what is there now? The Stone Roses? I don't think they've significantly changed anyone's life.
Q 1990

My new single is about how I got away from selling myself because of my looks and got on with what I'm best at and enjoy most – writing songs.
The Mirror 1990

I am not a meanie, or a miser, but I don't like charity gigs where the headline acts are just trying to boost their own image.
The Sun 1990

The funny part about all this speculation over my input and Andrew's was that between the two of us we got it sorted out very early on. In terms of the songwriting, Andrew just said off you go.
Today 1990

If you didn't have any self doubt you couldn't carry on. But I've become more confident and prolific which I hope to capitalise on. If you're a major selling artist these days you're not expected to make an album more than every two or three years. It's been three years since my last album and there's no way I want to do that any more. I want to make an album at least every 18 months, otherwise I don't think you grow and develop. In an ideal world, the business would divide into entertainers and musicians; entertainers would concentrate on live and video and visual work where the musicians would be nurtured and developed in the old sense of the word where they'd just make music and not bother with image.

I think there are a lot of people who want to listen to music but have their own visual images, their own interpretations. We've had ready made images served up with records for too long now and I believe people are beginning to get a bit sick of it. That's why I don't really like to discuss lyrics and what they're about because that takes away so much. It's like when you've had your heart broken and you hear a sad song on the radio; it's about you, not about the guy who sang it and his last broken romance. That's what love songs are all about.
Q 1990

I was aware that after Live Aid I was seen in some quarters as... a solo act. I was nervous as hell. It was the first time I had ever sung in front of an indifferent audience because every one I had sung in front of before had been mine – or ours. The miners' benefit wasn't

Above: George with Elton John

Below: with Bob Geldof.

an indifferent audience – that was hostile! But that was okay –
I did the miners' benefit because that was what I believed in, and
I knew what we could expect from the audience. So I was angered
by it, but I wasn't surprised. But with the Live Aid audience I knew
that I could be judged differently. More than anything, it showed
that people wanted me – quite unfairly – to do stuff on my own so
that they could admit to liking me. Everybody raved about my
performance, which I honestly thought was very average.

The interpretation I did of 'Don't Let The Sun Go Down On
Me' was very close to what Elton had done and I was out of tune
for the first couple of verses. I actually sing a lot better than that on
my records and I don't see why everyone should suddenly like me
just because I am there with musicians twice my age and I am taking
myself away from my friend. I didn't understand why that should be
suddenly credible. Live Aid was good for me but people's reaction
kind of annoyed me. It irritated me.
Bare 1990

I've become much more cynical about benefits now. I had a horrible
feeling about the people watching that Nelson Mandela show and
what they would feel about African acts. Half of them were there to

see Simple Minds and the other half were real thugs. I didn't like
the whole thing. What I wanted to do was separate myself from any
kind of self-promotion, I wanted to do something that would have
nothing to do with anything that I was selling at the time. I didn't
want to choose any material that had an overtly political message
because I thought it would come across as really naff coming from
me. So I thought the most political thing I could do was sing three
soul records by artists who had influenced me. Stevie Wonder,
Marvin Gaye, Gladys Knight. There was no other way I could have
done it and still felt comfortable, and it was a great opportunity
because you don't often get a chance to do those things for a valid
reason. Usually, people would think it's self indulgence. As it was,
a lot of people criticised me and said they were bored and would
have preferred to hear 'Father Figure' or 'One More Try' – very few
people thought it was a good idea.
Bare 1990

The idea of writing themes for soundtracks has interested me
for a long time. I've actually got a couple of pieces of music that I'm
waiting for the right project to use.
Chancery High Court 1993

For 'Faith' obviously I worked very hard, and I thought ultimately
it had negative effects on my life and my voice actually, so I don't
think that I would be touring with that intensity again. I don't see
myself being able to go through a tour of that length again, but no
doubt I will do fairly extensive tours in the future.
Chancery High Court 1993

I think it would be fair to say that I have not taken an interest in the industry in terms of promotion, but I think it would also be fair to say that I have taken a very great interest in the promotion of my own music. I am talking of artwork, packaging, interviews, videos – that type of thing.
Chancery High Court 1993

I don't mind television where I have a chance to mix the music after I've performed it. It was okay on the Freddie Mercury Tribute, for instance, but then I re-mixed it and it came out as a video with the single and it was far, far superior. I don't think with live television you have any assurances as to the quality of the perceived performance.
Chancery High Court 1993

Everyone's really got fed up with listening to people or celebrities slapping each other on the back for how generous they're being, and how they're donating their time and money, etc. etc. – and I don't blame them. I think we've saturated pop music with charity. And I don't think the people really believe in the people that they watch now when this kind of thing happens.
1993

It (The Freddie Mercury Tribute Concert) was the only charity event that I had participated in since Live Aid that had a total feeling of sincerity about it. It was probably the proudest moment of my career, because it was me living out a childhood fantasy, I suppose, to sing one of Freddie's songs in front of 80,000 people.
1993

The Man

I'm very analytical and pragmatic about myself. Sometimes I wish I were more instinctive but I put all the freer aspects of my personality into my music. I'm probably far too old for my years but I'm glad I've grown up quickly because it means I can enjoy the rest of my life more. Growing up's not very enjoyable.
Sunday 1987

If a nutter tried to polish me off, he could do it quite easily. It wouldn't make any difference if I had a bodyguard, because if somebody wanted to hurt me they could easily get a gun into a concert. It's not the kind of thing I worry about, because if you do have that sort of presence with you it will automatically make people very aggressive. Besides, I'm a very private guy and I couldn't bear to have somebody with me all the time.
Today 1987

It's true that I've lived a wild life but my days of going totally over the top have finished. Generally, it's unfair of people to expect you to be anything but human. OK, I used to get drunk a lot, but I'm not the type of person who throws his weight around. I get drunk very harmlessly and I've nothing to be ashamed of in the time I really did drink, other than the abuse of my body.
Today 1987

The more people you employ, the more people you have in your life who can't be honest with you and that's what I find most distressing about touring. You're responsible for so many people's livelihoods. I prefer to be with unbiased company, put it that way. People are terrified of me. I don't know why. I very rarely fire people. They'd have to do something really out of order. I'm very friendly to people but ... I really don't know why they're frightened of me. Maybe it's the size of my position. I'm quite distant even from the band, but I find it very distressing to get close to people who can't really be honest with me. I like to know that if I make a joke and the room laughs that it was funny. I'm not saying that anybody really licks my arse but it's evident, when you really analyse it, that at the end of the day I pay their wages. It frightens me. Being around people who can't tell you to fuck off. Whereas the people I spend time with in my personal life tell me to fuck off on a very regular basis!
Q 1988

I don't care what anyone says, I am not ashamed about the way I live.
1988

I must admit I go out less and less, now and then I have to go to pretty well the same places – where I know I'll get a bit of breathing space. But I think if you can come through Wham! and the exceptional exposure we had around '84 and '85 and you still have a social life, still go out and get pissed out of your head, then you're doing OK, you know. My big problem is I haven't got the ability to tell people to fuck off. I have the right to tell people to leave me alone. But it's not worth it to me now to be in a roomful of people and by the end of the evening five or six people have a real aggression toward you. I'd rather just be pleasant and tell people nicely. When I'm on tour I don't have any protection so I'm either rude to people and end up with everyone hating me, or I'm polite and waste my evening answering the same questions over and over. So I tend to get pissed out of my head and just try to enjoy myself. It is getting harder and harder but I think compared to a lot of people I still get out quite a lot on my own.

Q 1988

I was barred from Ascot racecourse when I turned up without a tie. They eventually let me in, but I was asked to stand at the back – worst thing was that I was wearing a £300 suit!

The Sun 1990

I never raised my voice to anyone on the whole tour. I never pulled anybody up. We had one member on the tour who got out of his brain on heroin a couple of nights and couldn't play, and I never said a word to him. The worst I ever did with him – and he knew he was almost out – was to tell him that I was going to trust him that it wasn't going to happen again.

Bare 1990

I've taken it. Loads of Ecstasy. I just don't do it any more. I took it when I was really depressed about five years ago, the first time I went to LA in Wham! It's not a great thing to do when you're depressed, that's why I stopped taking it. I don't benefit. I don't escape with drugs. Pretty well the same as I don't escape with booze. If I have a problem, it's there with me and I can't get rid of it by drinking or taking drugs. All Ecstasy used to do was intensify it the other end. It was virtually a different drug then, too, you have to remember. When I first took Ecstasy it was still a prescribed drug, the tablets had writing on. It's different now, half a pint of speed and a lot of other rubbish. I really don't get anything out of it any more, it was just a phase, although I couldn't say I'd never take it again because I don't know. What I'm glad about is that most of the people I know who took loads of Ecstasy came out of it and went on to coke, which is always a no-no for me. It's such a horrible drug. The only times in my life when I took it I had the most awful depressions and I didn't get any particular high off it either, so I just decided it wasn't for me and steered clear of it. The other awful thing about coke is people become such arseholes on it.

The thing I liked about Ecstasy was that it was your own decision which you made at the beginning of the night and once you'd done it, you'd done it. If you'd made a mistake then you were fucked, but you couldn't undo it, especially in those days as it was so strong there was never a question of having to do any more. But what I always hated and still hate about coke is the way it makes people behave. There's no privacy about it. They need some more so they'll suck up to someone they don't like or they'll be going on to some party that they don't want to go to. Women get fucked so they can do it, so do blokes. It's just the most sleazy drug. I'm so glad I never got into it. If I'd liked the stuff I may have been more tempted and it may have been a problem but I really didn't get on with it all the few times I tried.

Q 1990

When I came into this business I really had no idea that I was going to be any kind of idol. I was a particularly unattractive adolescent and what made it worse was that my partner in Wham! Andrew Ridgeley was very handsome. I assumed that he would get most of the attention and that is what happened first. Then things changed and I began to realise people didn't regard me as a Quasimodo. It was an odd feeling for someone who had been a fat boy with glasses who couldn't look at himself in the mirror. Suddenly, there were all these girls who wanted to go to bed with me and I got carried away. I slept with an awful lot of them.
The Mirror 1990

I've always had a feeling inside me that I won't live a long life – even though there's no heart trouble in my family or anything.
The Sun 1990

I started to feel far less that I was misplaced in my role. If people want to tell you you're good looking, what's the point in disagreeing.
Daily Express 1990

At work I am definitely bossy. I just can't help it. However, I don't tell people what to do outside work.
Daily Express 1990

Everyone has a sex life, and basically they are all pretty similar. I can have a laugh about some of the stories that are printed about me, but eventually you get sick of it.
Daily Express 1990

I think the main problem is that I am extremely suspicious of most people I meet. The clever thing to do would be to try and ignore that feeling, but once that suspicion is there it's ridiculously hard to

get rid of it. I don't actually meet that many people any more.
Daily Express 1990

I have got total confidence in my ability to control my destiny.
I have always felt that. When I wanted Wham!'s audience to change,
I knew I could do it.
Daily Express 1990

In general my life's fine. In fact, since the tour ended I've enjoyed
myself more than at any time I can remember. I've really come to
grips with what it is I want. I've got to grips with my career and
realised what a motivating force the insecurities I came out of
childhood with were. I've faced them all and although you don't get
rid of them they can't push you in that irrational sense any more.
People who are huge stars are very irrational in their drives...
I've been thinking about this and in order to stop wanting more and
more people to love you, you have to come to the conclusion that
you're worth loving in the first place and most huge stars don't
believe that. In a sense, I now believe that I'm worth loving and
I don't need the world to tell me any more.
Q 1990

Oh, I drink... probably more than I ever have. I don't think
I get as drunk as I used to, which is a bad sign, but I love wine and
I really like to drink it when I have something to eat. Breakfast,
elevenses, you know. I used to drink to get drunk and I didn't really
care what it was but now I drink because I love the taste... which
is even dodgier really. The real problem is I don't get any kind of
hangover, so there's no real incentive not to overdo it. I've always
been a lovely drunk though. I never get aggressive or unpleasant.
I'm always pretty much in control when I'm drunk as well... unless
I get completely wasted. But I think I should be more careful
because I'm only 27 and I have a lifestyle that could let me drink
more and more.
Q 1990

Of all the people I know, I'm probably the least lonely person.
I'm very lucky. I've got very close friends, wonderful family. Yes,
the relationship I wanted has broken down. It was one of those
relationships that tail off... messily. I tried recently to rekindle it.

It didn't work. But I'm very optimistic. I'm not the type of person who thinks I'm going to sit here the rest of my life on my own.
Sunday Correspondent 1990

I've grown up in the last two or three years. One of the things that's been most pleasant about growing up is the ability to face things, to accept all kinds of things about yourself. For years I used to fight with my physical self-image. Having gone from being an unattractive... or being made to feel very unattractive as a child, I then went to a situation where I got this sudden confidence that I wasn't Quasimodo, and then suddenly I was a pop star. I had all these girls screaming at me and wanting to sleep with me. So I slept with a lot of them. Then I found myself in a much more uncomfortable position because I felt I was more aware of the way I looked. I was a huge star, but why? In the physical sense, why? I didn't look good enough to be a huge star. It was all right to say, Yes, I wasn't unattractive. But I knew the difference, for instance, between me and a male model. I was really uncomfortable with cameras. And now I've got to the stage where I realise that it's OK. So I'm not Robert Redford, but I'm fine. I look fine.
Sunday Correspondent 1990

I can honestly say that I never lost my temper until I was 22. And then for a period of about six or eight months before the end of Wham! I really lost it. But I was blowing up in areas where normally I wouldn't. I was feeling paparazzi pressure.
Daily Mail 1990

I still get hurt but I try to keep those feelings in their place, I don't let them preoccupy me the way they used to. These outbreaks of emotion and weakness and feeling down have their place. I get on with life. And getting on with life is a lot easier for me than it is for other people.
Bare 1990

I'm quite self destructive. That's caused a lot of pain. You don't necessarily fall for people you want.
News World 1991

I'm not an arrogant person, but I have a real inner confidence. I really am an optimist.
Daily Express 1994

I felt I was losing control. More frightening was the feeling I had become distant from people, even my closest friends.
Daily Mirror 1994

The Image

I am not a Madonna or a Boy George. I am not a natural all day performer. Some people like them are. People seem to think we are, and that we should be something of great importance off stage or something very glamorous. I imagine people have made this mistake because on stage and on video we are very much actors. We obviously act well, because people believe there is something larger than life about us. But this is not the case.
1986

I used to feel to justify my position I had to be very good looking, but now I know that's got nothing to do with it. I still don't like looking at myself in films or pictures because I look chubby, but I've just got a round face. I've come to terms with that.
Today 1987

The hairdryer was working overtime in autumn, 1984, when I was sporting the baroque hairdo with the sculpted, blond locks. Some people thought I had the same hairdresser as Princess Diana. Some days I made the covers of the tabloids. Some days Princess Di made the covers of the tabloids. Some days I think they just got us mixed up.
Daily Mail 1990

I really yearned to be an ordinary guy. I was even paranoid about meeting people for the first time, worrying whether they wanted to talk to me because of who I am and not what I am. Then, one night, I got absolutely drunk and poured everything out. It was like an exorcism. The next morning I woke up and felt great. Now I've realised I should be grateful for my lot and that the grass isn't greener on the other side. It's green where I am. But without going through that period, I wouldn't be so happy now.
Today 1987

All through my career I have tried to project myself in a sexual manner. That must be trying to make up for something within myself. I don't see that person any more in the mirror. But I know that deep inside I am still making up for that fat kid.
Daily Express 1988

I saw a clip from 'Wake Me Up Before You Go Go' recently and I thought who the fuck is that? What the fuck am I trying to prove? I've never really been quite sure who in the audience goes for this look. When we started Wham! with denims and leathers, it was all

definitely very ambiguous because there were two of us and we had a very strong gay following. My whole character has always been fairly ambiguous to people anyway.
Q 1988

I'm no sex symbol. I'm a serious musician. I feel now that I am comfortable with my position as an artist, as a musician, and my status as a musician in this country. I feel that had the same effort been put around the world I would feel the same way about my worldwide situation. I've had so many friends whether they be bi or gay or straight or whatever, I'm so used to speculation. To tell you the truth it's never really bothered me. Lies bother me. Whether or not people say I'm gay doesn't bother me.
Q 1988

If people have got this image of me romping around in bed with Arnold Schwarzenegger, I'm not going to spoil their fun. I don't suppose he'd be too happy about it.
Sunday Correspondent 1990

I don't demand that friends treat me completely as though I were not George Michael. Because I am.
Sunday Correspondent 1990

The rock 'n' roll industry still lives with this romantic notion that if you are completely fucked up in everything other than your music, then your music is more beautiful and raw. If you are not aware of the business trappings, then it makes the centre much more real. It's bollocks. I'm just too together for people. They say I'm not very interesting. They just want some real contradictions. I'm sorry that I'm not Keith Richards or that I'm not born of the Sixties. I'm an Eighties pop star. It's not the same business. You can do all these things and be successful and manipulate all the other areas.
The Times 1990

When it first got to the stage that people were saying I was a sex symbol, I used to think this is a new one. I am certainly not worthy of being called that. Then I thought it was stupid and I almost felt like apologising to people when they met me.
Daily Express 1990

Initially, I loved the idea of being a sex object. Life as a heart throb became a six year distraction. In the end, it dawned on me that having people think you were gorgeous was not the most important thing in the world.
The Mirror 1990

I won't be doing any interviews or videos for the foreseeable future. I'm moving out of the promotional, selling myself side of things. Because that's what interviews always are. It's pure sell. I'm stopping because I just realised that it makes me unhappy. The person that I think I was when I started is not the same person as I am now. It's a difficult thing to explain... but the period when most people grow up, I didn't. I went from school to being a pop star, which isn't real, life and my growing up period happened quite late – in the last three years. Now I've realised that I don't want to sell myself any more and not just that, I don't really want to be visible anymore. I still really love making music and I still want people to like my music. But I want them to like it for what it is. I'm not overly concerned about selling millions and millions of records.
Q 1990

I've realised that I have a lot more respect for my own music than I used to have. I actually believe in what I do as a musician now, divorced completely from the imagery. And I've come to the point where I know that creating imagery makes me unhappy now. What I didn't want to do was just suddenly stop and step back and try and create some sort of mystique. I want people to know that for the foreseeable future, unless there's something really important to say – which I don't think there will be – I'm going to kind of disappear. I've made a platform for myself now from which I can make music and that's all. It's not me going, oh I'm such a serious musician who takes himself so seriously that people should only hear the music. It's just now I think the music is strong enough to stand up on its own... and my priority now is to keep myself happy.
Q 1990

I'm constantly reading people's opinions of me and they're not that good in general. I've never really been able to work from a position where people are very sympathetic with me simply because I've always been successful in this country, you're constantly defending yourself. And when you're defending yourself you do find that you're analysing your motives for this, your reasons for that. I have to be careful not to absorb too much of the aggression I get towards me in the press. But I've always been pretty self-analytical and my songs have always been like that. But then I'm probably a lot of things I wouldn't have been had I not become famous.
Q 1990

I'm still seen, in some areas as some lightweight little pop singer. It's the complete opposite in America. If anything they take me a bit too seriously. They think I'm this really serious moody bloke.
Q 1990

Once I was with Shirlie Holliman coming out of Stringfellow's and these two photographers jumped in front of us and the flashes just seemed to set me off. I grabbed this guy and pushed him up against the wall – it was just so unlike me, being macho. I started swearing at him, threatening to kill him. The other guy got a picture of me, just as I turned with a really nasty expression on my face.
Daily Mail 1990

I decided to take some time off and reconsider. I was just incredibly depressed. I wasn't doing anything other than getting away from the situation, getting away from the people, business – just travelling around, trying to have a good time – although I wasn't having a good time.
Daily Mail 1990

Once I used to feel like a fraud. I used to think that there was an element of me that, some day, everyone was going to wake up to – and that everything would be taken away, the bottom would just fall out of my world. And that's just gone now. The fear has gone. I no longer feel like this is a stage in my life. This is my life and not a rehearsal for it. The challenge now is to stay successful and... happy. I keep fame in a little box and sometimes I take it out and enjoy it. The reason I'm successful is because I have a gift – but it's not indestructible and I have to protect it.

Daily Mail 1990

In the future I don't intend to show myself the way I have in the past, I will no longer promote and talk to the media the way I did in the past, I don't intend to stare the world in the face any more. I'll always make records because I love music. But I don't enjoy being in the business, I don't enjoy the hardening process that has already begun, that I can already feel in myself. I look at people who have been in the business for a long time, and I know I don't want to be like them.

Bare 1990

The look on stage, that kind of arrogance, is like putting on clothes for me. It's exactly the same thing when I go out – it's an act. In person, it's a defence mechanism. On stage, it's an entertainment mechanism. Because the person in the videos doesn't really exist. The songwriter does. And the songs exist. That's all real. But the person in the videos doesn't really exist.

Bare 1990

I got the jeans from Woodhouse, the T-shirt and socks
from Marks and Spencer, and the red cheeks from an over-zealous
make-up artist.
Bare 1990

A huge insecurity is obviously the motivating force for most artists.
And I understand that. But I feel that it's dangerous on a personal
level to have a huge gap between what you are in your work and
what you are in reality.
Bare 1990

It wouldn't matter if I met someone and fell hopelessly in love
with them and they felt the same about me, I would still always be
the pop star George Michael to them. Even though they would get
underneath that image, a part of them would always perceive me
that way.
Daily Mail 1990

Late in the autumn of 1986 I changed my mind about carrying on,
about promoting, about playing the game. I felt that I had wasted
most of the year feeling sorry for myself. I basically decided that
I would do it all again. But this time it would be on my terms.
Bare 1990

The actual video of 'Faith' is the strongest image of me off the album – the jacket, the jeans, the boots – and I didn't think that was far enough away from the way I really dressed to believe in it as some big visual statement. I wasn't comfortable with how strong that image became – because ultimately it begins to blur the reasons for your success.
Bare 1990

When you look at 'The Final' album there are four or five images in there and each one shows a different year and a different look. I was still a kid trying to work out which way I looked best. Did my hair look best short or long? Dark or blond? with or without a beard? It wasn't a David Bowie thing – I wasn't changing to keep the people interested, I was always dissatisfied, never confident. And I'm just not going to make that effort to go out looking that different any more. It's okay if you're interested in that chameleon business and you want to do, for instance, what Madonna or Prince do – and they do it very well. But it's not for me.
Bare 1990

The 'Faith' image has a lot of restrained aggression in it. I don't think it's over the top aggression. It was the way I dressed at the time and very often still do – just a ripped pair of jeans, a leather jacket, those were the glasses I had been wearing, and the shoes too – and we just stylised it. Obviously I can't wear the whole outfit all together now because I would just look like a real wanker – a George Michael lookalike. I never considered it a particularly macho look but I tried to soften it just a bit by having a string of pearls on one of the shoulders of the leather jacket.
Bare 1990

Listen, Mike Tyson has been accused of being homosexual.
What chance do I have.
News World 1991

I have never felt any connection between the Greeks and me,
other than how hairy I am.
1991

I'm not an arrogant person, I don't think I'm particularly conceited,
but I have a real inner confidence that this is what I was meant to do
and that, whatever other failings I have, I am someone who has a
craft, an ability, which has incredible by-products. Because of that,
I never let situations get on top of me for any length of time.
I really am an optimist and I believe that what I do is a good thing,
a positive influence.
Bare 1990

I am perfectly aware of the level of importance of sexuality in
my career. I'm perfectly aware of it, but I don't honestly think that
I've created something to sell. I believe that I did what I was doing
at the time as a person and put it on film and I would not actually –
even though I totally acknowledge its importance – when I was
making the video for 'Faith' that was the way I was looking when
I was walking about in the street. When I stopped looking like that
in my real life, I stopped looking like that on video. What I am
saying is, I totally acknowledge the importance of it but I didn't
engineer it – I was looking the way I wanted to look as a young
man and I don't think that I actually engineered individual looks for
the public any more than I did for my own self or for my own
insecurities.
Chancery High Court 1993

They (some stars) are afraid of the stigma that's attached to Aids.
I'm not afraid of the association at all, people might think well, this
person is campaigning for Aids on a regular basis – this must mean
he's gay. It's really sad to me that people think in order to work
towards a cure you have to be afflicted yourself, but in my own
mind it makes no difference to me.
1993

I haven't done very many interviews since the alarming amount of
money that I supposedly am worth has been quoted, and I think I've
totally left it up to other people to speculate.
Chancery High Court 1993

I was eighteen years old and I worked my way through my early
twenties looking the way and changing the way I wanted to look

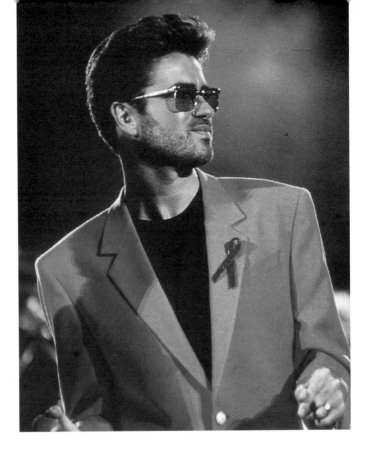

just based on my own view of myself.
Chancery High Court 1993

I think I drastically changed my physical image when I recorded the live duet with Elton (John). It was a much more toned-down very unsexual performance.
Chancery High Court 1993

I think that the reaction of fans is roughly the same everywhere. I think that the age group of fans was slightly different in America simply because my career began in America two years later than it did in the rest of the world.
Chancery High Court 1993

George with Elton John.

It's a very strange term "superstar". It doesn't qualify anything.
Chancery High Court 1993

I actually felt that the UK company were aware of the fact that I had successfully manoeuvred myself into a position where I could be seen as an adult-orientated artist.
Chancery High Court 1993

If I step outside the promotion and marketing of George Michael, then I think I have every chance of surviving as a successful musician and a balanced human being. I've achieved every other goal. I've done just about everything that I could – and that's my goal now.
Sunday Times 1993

Sex, Love & Relationships

I was making up for lost time because I didn't get much sex when I was a kid. Not many people were attracted to me and the ones that were, were almost always ugly.
Sunday 1987

I don't think people have the right to know whether I'm a spank freak, gay, bisexual, totally straight or celibate. I don't believe in knowing what people do in bed because I don't care what other people do in bed. I've got enough problems with what I do in bed.
Sunday 1987

It's impossible to have a successful relationship when you're sleeping around. In my situation, you meet an awful lot of women who aren't typical. They play on the worst aspect of men's characters. Sex is for both sides but these women get a lot more than sex. They get possessions and the glamour of being associated with a star. I've been used like this and it hurt. But I've learnt pretty quickly. It's the kind of thing people don't learn for years. If I seem old for my years then I'm glad because I've made mistakes early enough to rectify them and can enjoy the rest of my life without making them again. Because I've been in close proximity with so many women who have no pride in themselves, I admire women who have dignity and respect for themselves and their sexuality.
Today 1987

I'll only get married when I want to be a dad. Without a family I think marriage is a pointless exercise. And as far as I'm concerned I cannot afford to have kids until I've fulfilled my ambitions. It's no good being a part-time dad. I would want to be a full-time dad and not travelling all over the world promoting things.
Today 1987

I got a great kick when I first met Kathy (Yeoung) because she didn't like me, and wasn't impressed by me. I know she would never make money from our relationship. She gets quite bugged about being known as George Michael's girlfriend. Kathy's an original girl, and fun to be with.
Today 1987

I've got nothing to hide, I'm not gay.
1988

There's now a new morality. In the past there was an argument for and against casual sex. These days it can be a matter of life or death. I went through bedhopping and all the rest of it, but I don't need that to boost my sexual ego.

Daily Mail 1988

Marriage comes down to whether you love somebody enough. I don't know whether I've met that person.

Daily Mail 1988

Bedhopping no longer appeals. Though, strangely, for some people it lasts forever. You see 35 to 45 year old guys who are still doing it. The novelty has worn off, though changing my lifestyle has nothing to do with Aids. It's simply to do with getting older and finding a relationship you are happy with.

Daily Express 1988

I have found it very difficult to share my own space with anybody. But eventually, it comes down to whether you love someone enough to sacrifice that space.

Daily Express 1988

I believe that if you are sleeping with a lot of girls you don't develop much as a person. My relationship with Kathy changed me a lot. I've developed. I've become more directed and positive. I can concentrate more on my career and the things that are important to me without having the distraction of looking for something.

Today 1989

Men are not used to being hunted. Initially, I thought it was absolutely wonderful. I really thought it was fantastic. And I abused the privilege a little bit maybe – although I wasn't getting anything out of a sexual situation that wasn't being returned. In fact, it got to the point where I realised that I was getting less out of it than they were and that starts to be a turn off.
Bare 1990

The things that get me down – like the lack of freedom or wanting to be in the right relationship or wanting an old relationship back – can only take up a certain amount of my energy these days, whereas they used to take up most of it.
Daily Mail 1990

Now I'm so aware of the fact that I'm a catch. The women are not the catch. I am the catch. It's not a very attractive feeling for me. Andrew doesn't mind at all. Andrew loves it! But I'm not really into being the catch.
Bare 1990

Obviously the thing that's missing from my life is a stable relationship. But I don't wake up thinking I wish I was sharing my life with somebody. I've changed. Two or three years ago when I saw young guys in the park with their kids, I had this incredible sense of envy. It's gone. I don't know what's happened to it but it's gone.
Daily Mail 1990

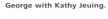

George with Kathy Jeuing.

To me a successful relationship is where two people can live and exist happily together but still change and evolve. My parents are in their fifties and they've changed so much over the last ten years. A successful relationship is where the evolution of two people is allowed. But that's where people go wrong. They marry each other and are pretty much compatible, and then one of them goes off in one direction and the other either stays where they are or goes off in an opposing direction or they just can't accept changes. People do change. Their life experiences change them. It's good, that's how it should be, but I do think that's the greatest difficulty about people living together.

Daily Mail 1990

George with parents Jack and Lesley Panayiotou.

I think people staying together is the way it should be. I just don't know if that's what I'm going to have. I can't imagine living with someone. I would normally think that's okay because everybody feels like that until they meet the right person, but I have a horrible feeling that part of the pleasure of living on my own is that my need for privacy is so much greater than most people's.

Daily Mail 1990

I can be interested when you are exchanging looks across a room, but it's different when someone just sidles up and propositions you. It's not a very masculine position – obviously most men are comfortable being the ones who do the chasing.
Bare 1990

The black time ended after I had it out with Andrew, that time of feeling sorry for myself and thinking that everything was a pile of shit. He made me see how wrong that was. I'm just as close to some other people as I am to Andrew, but it's a different kind of relationship and he understands things about me on an intellectual level that the others don't, even though in some ways they know me much better. I hadn't seen him for quite a while and he was the person I needed to talk to. It was the beginning of the turn around – so much so that when I saw him a few months later and told him that I was all right, he was still very worried about me and needed some convincing that I was really okay.
Bare 1990

I lost my virginity at 13. I remember thinking, what is all the fuss about? I was overweight and wore glasses – and was hopeless with women. She was a right old dog. I was so inexperienced that it was embarrassingly bad.
The Sun 1990

The idea of sex in Rock and Roll has always involved sex with a stranger, sex with someone you have just set eyes on. Rock and Roll comes with the idea that there is nothing at all erotic about your girlfriend or boyfriend. Sex is something that you really shouldn't be doing – that's how you get your pleasure from it. And that's not true. Everybody's ideal, certainly my ideal, is that fucking is best with someone that you feel good about, someone you know and want to be with and yet you can't keep your hands off them and you want to rip their clothes off. There's a lot of lust in that and there needs to be lust in a relationship.
Bare 1990

The one person I really wanted – the one I thought my life would revolve around – didn't want me. It hit me hard. The relationship screwed me up because I am usually the one who does the leaving. It was messy and I am used to being loved. It was unfair. It had nothing to do with me as a person, as an individual with two legs, eyes and dark hair. It had everything to do with me being a pop star. I was spoilt in so many ways – going straight from school into the band, having no money problems, being able to sleep with whoever I wanted whenever I wanted, and my career going exactly as I liked it – then someone pulled the carpet away. I drank myself stupid for months. I was in a very bad way and started losing my temper for the first time in my life. I got into fist fights with friends, threw photographers against walls and acted very macho.

Today 1990

There is no combination of sexual elements that I've ever thought were wrong. I have had so many friends – whether they be bisexual or gay or straight or whatever – it doesn't bother me. Anyway, what two people do in bed should be no concern of anybody else.

Today 1990

It would be nice to have anonymous sex, maybe. But maybe it would be terribly dull. Maybe if people weren't trying... ha!... it would be terribly dull. Like any other aspect of fame, it creeps up on you slowly. It comes up on you so slowly that you can't remember when it was different. I can't vaguely remember sex when it was anonymous.

Sunday Correspondent 1990

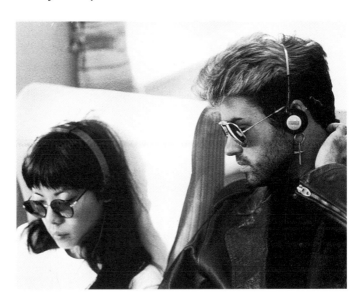

It's fucking difficult, I mean how do you normally work out
that someone is attracted to you if you go to a club or to a party?
You tell because they stare at you. Even if they don't want to, they
stare at you. I remember what that was like as a kid. I remember
the kick I got out of someone being attracted to me who I'd never
met before and... it takes a long time to learn the difference.
Because everyone's bloody staring at you. They don't all fancy you.
They may all want to go to bed with you, but it doesn't mean
they're all attracted to you.
Sunday Correspondent 1990

I've had three relationships, really, since the beginning of the thing.
I don't think I made a mistake. I don't think I've made a mistake
with friends either.
Sunday Correspondent 1990

I don't necessarily believe in love at first sight, but I believe in
the power of infatuation and what it can do to you. Even today,
I'm likely to have the same problem. Still, that's why, just in terms
of friends, the people who attract me have to be honest and
unimpressed.
Daily Mail 1990

It's easy to get sex in my position. There's no problem.
News World 1991

Maybe I could sleep with someone in disguise. If they didn't know
who I was, they might not try so hard in bed.
News World 1991

I have to be really convinced someone wants to sleep with me
as opposed to the person they think is me. I haven't taken advantage
of my status for a long time – the idea isn't attractive to me any
more. In the initial period of fame I went with a lot more people
than I'd ever been with before. Now, I have to be really convinced
someone wants to sleep with me to go to bed for the first time.
People don't stay with you all their lives because you're some pop
star. You know when someone's fallen in love with you.
Daily Mail 1991

Fame

I didn't know how much longer I could stand losing my privacy.
But it is all gone now. It is like having your life documented for
approval or disapproval, down to the minutest detail. We would
understand if we were Royalty, but we are not. It makes you feel
trivial. It can be a little embarrassing.
1986

People only have a certain amount of interest in one band for a
certain amount of time. They are not going to want to keep reading
what colour underpants I wear. Fortunately, there are always places
you can run to and escape this kind of thing. I will buy myself a
little island.
1986

The only paranoia that fame puts on you is the thought that you're
tomorrow's office gossip. There's that horrible feeling that goes with
one night stands of them getting more out of them than you.
Sunday 1987

Obviously, there are still certain things missing from my life.
Things like anonymity and the freedom to do what I want, when
I want, but they are the sort of things you give up for fame. I haven't
really had any adult life when I might have had them so I don't
miss them. I can't remember what it was like to be unknown.
There are still times when fame can be embarrassing and days when
I feel trapped but, generally, I'm perfectly happy to be recognised.
I go to the supermarket on my own. People gawk but if you need
bread you have to get it.
Today 1987

Music is my business and that's all I really care about right now.
1988

George Michael fans in Britain and Europe are still divided
between the people who are into what I do as a recording or
performing artist and the people who are into what I am physically.
In America it's fine for an adult, completely acceptable, to go into
a conversation and say, Have you heard the new George Michael
album? I think it's great. In England it's still dodgy. There's that
stigma. I've never been keen on the idea of having to sell myself as
an adult. As I say, in America it hasn't been necessary. I'm accepted
as an adult because the music has already done it. In England
I would love people to realise that there is a change, but the tabloids

and the limited TV and radio structures aren't letting people discover that for themselves.

Q 1988

In rock music you can be a real star as an intellect or a personality or an enigma. In my context I was someone who had a lot of confidence in myself as a writer but knew that I wasn't subversive or an exceptional person in any other way. I knew that there wasn't anything about me that would really fascinate people. Then suddenly it dawned on me that I could raise people's opinions of me as a physical entity. When that happened I threw myself into it completely and that led to the period of depression when I actually believed in that person that I'd created for the media. Now that performing or promotional persona is just like a magnified version of me but around '84 it wasn't the type of guy who could walk into a room and pull any bird, and suddenly, at 19, I could.

Q 1988

When I was 19 or 20 there were any number of fairly ordinary up to quite good-looking people I could take home. Now, if I chose to, I could walk into a room and leave with people who are much better looking or think a lot more of themselves. It's ironic really, now that I don't chose to, a lot of people are available to me. I find the idea of being that much of a catch for someone a very masculine and very castrating position to be in. There's no chase, you don't have to do anything.

Q 1988

I got asked to a thing at Kensington Palace a while ago and I didn't do it. I've got nothing against the Royals at all, I'm not anti-Royal. I just think that it's very dangerous for celebrities to get involved with Royalty. All the Royals I'd met have been very sweet. I think people who are anti-Royal don't realise how little remaining character England has.

The Mirror 1988

It's the most thrilling day of my life. I'm so proud, not only for me but for Britain and other British performers who won awards. I was asleep when my manager called to say I had won (the US Grammy for 'Faith'). It was about 7am and the phone hasn't stopped ringing since.
Daily Express 1989

Just because you are rich and famous it doesn't mean your life is problem free. My problems are not any greater or lesser than when I was 17. They're just different.
The Mirror 1990

Everyone likes to think that they will leave something behind when they die. At the end of the day I want to leave something as a writer.
Today 1990

Most people find it hard to believe that stardom can make you miserable. After all, everybody wants to be a star. I certainly did and I worked hard to get it. But I was miserable. I decided that the thing I really enjoyed, the thing I really needed, was my songwriting. I didn't need the celebrity. The truth is it all got much bigger than I ever imagined – and much harder to control. Ultimately I wasn't comfortable with that kind of visibility and power. If my life goes the way I want it to I would like never to step in front of a camera again.
The Sun 1990

You have to come to terms with all the things you can't do.
For example, I can't go shopping because of the danger of being
mobbed.
Daily Express 1990

When I came back (after being on tour) in '88 everyone was
completely out of it. So I missed most of the real heavy Ecstasy year.
People were kind of getting that way before I left but when I came
back there were people – who I thought would never touch the stuff
– absolutely out of their brains.
Q 1990

You have to be the type of person who can say no to everyone.
When I go out I start with the intention. But everyone that comes
up to you is different. I just can't give them a stock answer. With
some people I feel bad about giving them the brush-off, but with
others I take great pleasure in telling them to go away. I've got a set
reply now for fans asking for autographs. I smile quite nicely and
say "Sorry it's my night off", and it works – generally – because
I'm friendly about it. Signing things is something I do all the time,
so I would rather not be bothered when I'm out.
Daily Express 1990

I want to step back from all the self-publicity and promotion and
marketing to protect my ability, my gift as a songwriter. I think that
if I've abused that gift it's been by not using it enough. I want
to change that. I've realised I need to fight to protect that gift.
But even more than that, I need to protect my life.
Bare 1990

This business is so professional you can't get out of your skull all
the time – not if you want to keep your head above water. There are
people in the business that I know who are out of their skulls half
the time – but for every person like that there's someone waiting
to take their place, saying I'm not going to get into this rubbish.
Eventually those artists that don't take it seriously find themselves
out of money, they won't be able to write music properly and people
who were their friends will take the mickey.
Daily Express 1990

I think if I step outside the promotion and marketing of George
Michael, doing all the videos and the big tours and interviews, then
I have every chance of surviving as a successful musician and a
balanced human being. I've achieved every other goal, I've done just
about everything that I could and that's my goal now. I hope the
public understands. I don't want people to feel pissed off or to feel

that I've deserted them. I know that a lot of people feel loyal to me and I just want to make sure that I'm still giving them something worthwhile in ten years' time. But it doesn't take much courage to step back from this kind of fame.
Bare 1990

I'm not prepared to sacrifice my life just for my ego – I don't need to now. I used to be very excited by the thought of being a star, but I'm not driven by the old securities any more.
Daily Mail 1990

Celebrity fucks people up. Celebrity knocks the stuffing out of people, personally and creatively. There's not much that fucks you up faster than celebrity and isolation.
Bare 1990

I hate meeting celebrities. I've got a lot of time for Michael Jackson, he was very gracious to me when I won my award last year, but on the whole I don't enjoy meeting celebrities. Not because of what they are like as individuals but because the basis of your common ground is so flimsy. What can you say? "Oh, hello, so you're rich and famous too! Oh, so you're a celebrity too!" What the fuck are you supposed to talk about? It's quite difficult. I tend to be the one who goes up to someone and says – "Look, I really admire what you do". And it's always true, I never say it to someone I don't feel that way about – and I have laid myself open to some nasty experiences that have made me shy away from talking to celebrities. If it's at all possible, I stay away from the situation.
Bare 1990

I'm in the position now where I have the luxury of being able to do what I want but I've come to the conclusion that I've spent almost 10 years trying to convince myself and the world that I was something really special.
Q 1990

There are times when the fact that everyone is looking at you doesn't bother you and times when it does. I can honestly say that I wouldn't miss it. I'd miss the freedom it's brought me in that I can do what I want most of the time. If I couldn't fly off somewhere or get a table at a restaurant any time I wanted, those kind of perks, if they were taken away from me I'm sure I'd notice. As for being recognised, here people give me a bit more room now but at the moment in America I don't have that any more.
Q 1990

One thing that struck me recently is that I'm constantly met with smiles, because whenever I walk into a shop or see someone drive past in a car they're thinking, there's George Michael! I'll tell people about this tonight. I'll dine out on this one for a while. It's an experience. Therefore I get a very positive – although probably completely false – reaction from everyone I meet. You forget that that's not a normal experience and that most people are met with indifference. I'm never met with indifference. People always come towards me smiling.
Q 1990

I know why people are nice to me – they're meeting a famous person – and I'm not stupid enough to think everyone likes me because they come up smiling. But it does make you demand that much more from individuals if you're going to allow them to get anywhere near close to you. I've developed an ability to work out,

very quickly, whether or not people are genuine. I feel I really have
to get a sense of trust from someone to even allow them past the
most superficial level. I've got a fairly good intuition about people.
I haven't been had-over or taken by surprise in the last four or five
years. I've made friends and they've all been good friends and
I've worked out who I should steer clear of.
Q 1990

I came out of Wham! with not very much at all and I came
out of the whole 'Faith' thing with a hell of a lot. It sold somewhere
between 13 or 14 million, which is quite phenomenal if you think
about getting all those people in one place. It doesn't bear thinking
about. But that's the modern music industry. Imagine what The
Beatles would have sold if they had known about marketing then.
If you could integrate a pop group into the progression of a whole
generation these days like The Beatles and the Stones in the Sixties,
the numbers would be frightening. They were a huge cultural
phenomenon but people just don't know how to sell them properly.
It's different now. Madonna isn't a cultural phenomenon and neither
am I and neither is Jackson. We're sales phenomenons.
Q 1990

It's like the guy impersonating me on that *Stars In Their Eyes*.
I haven't seen that one but I saw the week before and they had
people doing Shirley Bassey, John Lennon and I thought, how come
I fit into that area? It's a weird thing because you've almost moved
into some sort of folklore. I find that ridiculous and I really don't
understand how that's happened. It's a strange thing to have
happened to you. In a way I suppose it should make you feel secure
knowing that you're so famous, people will never forget who you
are but when you've become part of the old establishment at 27 you
start thinking. Hang on...
Q 1990

Madonna is trapped in the way that Jackson's become trapped.
And that was my next option. There's a point of no return, and
I think I've stopped just short of it. I'm lucky, I know, because I still
live the life I want to live. I do what I like. I still travel about.
I'm quite sure Madonna can't remember the last time she travelled
from country to country on her own – or Jackson, or Prince.
Obviously this isn't an ordinary life. But I do normal ordinary
things, and I know, with time, I'll be able to do more and more
ordinary things. If I don't do that much promotion... if you don't
push, it gets easier.
Sunday Correspondent 1990

She'll (Madonna) be hounded for ever now. And Jackson.
In terms of what their ultimate objective is – which very definitely
is a kind of immortality – they should finish themselves off somehow
now. The only way Madonna is going to get closer to Marilyn
Monroe is to top herself.
Sunday Correspondent 1990

In pursuing stardom, I've wasted a lot of time. I don't think I'd
realised how meaningless chasing the celebrity circuit was until I'd
taken it as far as I could. In the Eighties you didn't have to do much
more than keep repeating what you had done and, as long as your
youth was holding up and you're not letting anybody down age wise,
you don't have to worry about much more than that.
The Times 1990

I just wanted the attention of thousands of women I suppose. I was
a very insecure child. Most huge stars are driven by these insecurities. I wasn't that attractive and I just had this feeling that if I could
become a pop star I could make up for my shortcomings. What
happened was that at some point I realised I could do a lot more
than that – you could take yourself to a level where you are almost
untouchable, which I suppose, is where I am.
The Times 1990

I keep fame in a little box and sometimes I take it out and
enjoy it. I don't think you can survive more than a certain amount
of superstardom before it starts affecting you – and the people around
you – in very sad and clichéd ways. The reason I'm successful
is because I have a gift – but it's not indestructible and I have to
protect it.
Bare 1990

I was at my other home in Santa Barbara recently. It's so peaceful,
so serene there, so natural. You've got eagles flying around the

house, chipmunks all over the place, you can step outside the door and pick oranges, lemons, all kinds of fruit. And it suddenly occurred to me – this is what rich people spend their money on. It wasn't a comfortable feeling for me. This was never about money.
Bare 1990

I used to be able to feel sorry for myself for very long periods of time. But when I feel like that now, I look at the things that I have. You only have to walk down the street to see the desperation of other people's situations and you only have to look at their faces to see how tired some people are of life. You can get away from your problems, but I just line mine up against other people's and find that they're not that difficult to deal with.
Daily Mail 1990

I don't feel the need to be a star any more.
Daily Mail 1991

I have a horrible feeling that part of my pleasure of living on my own is that my need for privacy is so much greater than other people's. I feel a very great need to be away from George Michael most of the time.
Sunday Times 1993

They play my songs on Coronation Street.
Chancery High Court 1993

Money

I don't get any pleasure out of money in terms of what it can buy for me. I have comforts and I have security. But to me it is something quite irrelevant. I am not an extravagant person. I don't buy lots of clothes. I put it all back into my career.
1986

Money does give you a lot of confidence. I know that no one can ever pull the rug out from under me. I am worth a lot of money and I know I can spend it on what I like today and it won't affect my pocket tomorrow. It's an incredible freedom to have. Money is such a big problem in most people's lives, but it is a problem I am lucky enough to have avoided.
Today 1987

My only extravagance is cars. I spend a lot of money on them because they're like toys to me. And I buy clothes for prices I wouldn't have dreamt of paying years ago.
Today 1987

I love having money, it brings you good times and happiness. People who say it doesn't are lying.
Today 1988

I think the music business pays individuals an awful lot of money for doing something which is, basically, a pleasure to do, but I don't feel guilty about it.
Today 1988

It's very strange, I've not really noticed the difference between being rich and being very rich. I've been as free as money can make you for a long time. When you don't have to think about money, one thing it can do to you is give you too much time to think about other things, so you can develop a whole new set of problems – which I suppose I have done to an extent.
Q 1988

When I have friends who have money problems I try and get their perspective on it because you really do forget what it's like. Then I normally end up lending them money anyway! Everyone owes me money. And they all say, you're the last person to come and ask for it back. So I'll probably be owed it for a long time. The best thing about being rich is I could spend a ridiculous amount of money now and know that it would have no effect on my life

next week or next year. I'm extravagant in the sense that I go
through a lot of hi-fi equipment. I'm always getting the latest stuff.
And one thing that I really have developed a liking for that costs a lot
of money is... um... drugs. Ha ha Ha. No it's not. It's cars actually.
It's a real cliché, isn't it? It's a toy. But overall I get something from
people and I get something from music, but things in themselves
hold no real value for me. I'm not a possession-orientated person,
but I swear if I lost every penny tomorrow I'd be rich again within
two years. Even if I couldn't do it for myself. Writing songs is
my bank.
Q 1988

Let's face it, all the musicians who reach my level of success are
vastly overpaid.
Today 1988

I have been reported to have a conspicuous spending pattern but
I probably spend an alarmingly small amount compared with most
people in my situation.
Today 1988

I am very happy it's over (Libel against *The Sun* newspaper).
It's not as much as the £1 million Elton John got from *The Sun*,
but it is a six-figure sum. I will be giving it to separate charities for

the mentally handicapped. I am currently working on a new album, but have no plans to tour just yet.
Daily Express 1989

I love having money and I'm not afraid to say it. Of course I'm richer than most 24 year olds, but I don't consider myself stinking rich. Sometimes I can spend £3,000 on clothes just in an afternoon. But what I really love doing is writing songs.
Today 1989

The money has never been an essential part of it. I came into this business with no money, so right from the start it seemed like I was earning a lot. It was not so much where's my money, but a question of who's getting my money instead of me?
Daily Express 1990

I love England. Tax-wise it's very expensive here but I couldn't give a toss really. I've got more money than I know what to do with anyway. I can't pretend that I need any more money or that I need to hang on to my tax money. I've always paid my full tax. In the Wham! days people were always saying, take a year out of the country... but I just don't see the point in having money if you're not where you want to be. It makes the world an open prison if you can't wake up somewhere you want to be. What's money for, you know?
Q 1990

I think I've made vast amounts of money because I make music which appeals to a very large audience and because there is now a network, a marketing network which allows all of those people to buy that music. I think it's a combination.
Chancery High Court 1993

I have given away a substantial percentage of what I am worth.
Chancery High Court 1993

The problem with this country is that it's falling apart and the average working class person has nothing. If they're lucky, people have only just enough money to put a bit of food in their fridge and a little petrol in the car.
Sunday Express, June 1994

I hate giving so much money to a Government I don't approve of, but I don't think making money is a Right wing act in itself. If life was fair then I think people who get all the money would be those who spent their lives doing things for other people.
Today 1988

The Court Case

Sony Music has a clear and unwavering commitment to
George Michael. Together, our relationship with him has been
mutually fruitful. Our contract with George is valid and legally
binding. We are saddened and surprised by the action George has
taken. There is a serious moral as well as legal commitment attached
to any contract, and we will not only honour it, but vigorously
defend it.
Sony Music, The Independent 1992

George with Dick Leahy.

His (George Michael) dispute is not about ego or money.
George has enough money for all his needs. It's about the style of
management. Under the old management there was an understanding
that their top worldwide artists would develop over time, and change
direction when they needed to. Now it's all short-term thinking.
All a record company has to do is market what he gives them, and
he feels he wasn't marketed adequately. He feels Sony got their
priorities wrong and made a lot of mistakes.
Dick Leahy, George Michael's music publisher & confidant,
The Independent 1992

Since the Sony Corporation bought my contract, I have seen the
great American music company that I proudly signed to as a teenager
become a small part of the production line for a giant electronics
corporation. Musicians do not come in regimented shapes and sizes,
but are individuals who change and evolve together with their
audiences. Sony obviously views this as a great inconvenience.
The Independent 1992

Basically the main thrust of my disappointment in Sony UK at the
time... I think how they spent their money was that they sustained
regional advertising on the album, and I was shocked that there was
no advertising going on in London, and I was shocked that they had
not promoted the B-side that I had prepared to help them in the
charts with 'Waiting For That Day'. So I would say totally...
I obviously didn't feel at the time that they were totally committed.
Chancery High Court 1993

I found it surprising that for their biggest selling artist they waited
before they advertised in London, which presumably has got to be
one of the strongest areas. I must admit even though they did a very
good job over the course of the album around the country, I was
surprised that they felt they had to test areas before they could spend
money in London.
Chancery High Court 1993

My reason for wanting to part with Sony is because I don't believe that one particular area of the world which is very important to me has any belief in me or any motivation to exploit my work.
Chancery High Court 1993

If there's a relationship between artist and record company it should be a mutual thing. If an artist wants certain songs on the radio I would have thought the record company's position with that artist, especially after almost ten years, would be to try and support that.
Chancery High Court 1993

I decided to take two months or so off of working on that album. ('Listen Without Prejudice Volume II') was very much – the huge success of the duet with Elton (John) convinced me that actually my market was – that I had to make a decision of sorts and that it was possible that the transition that I had been waiting for was pretty much achieved and that my next album should – I was very torn between the two markets and I like to work musically in ... and I decided at that stage... the Elton single convinced me that I was going to have to abandon the idea of going full pelt promoting myself as a dance artist. But I didn't abandon the album. You have to remember also that Sony UK had expressed very definitely that they were in no hurry to release 'Volume II' and that they felt that even though it would have fulfilled the promise that I had made to them – there was plenty of time and that I could possibly be over-exposed with various things that were in the charts at the time. So they weren't desperate for this – Sony UK at least weren't desperate for this, and as far as I was concerned, I was going to take two months off, come back to it and complete it once again as an adult orientated album.
Chancery High Court 1993

My criticism of CBS UK is not... I'm not really complaining. I am saying that I was satisfied with the job they did and that even though I do believe that the more extensive advertising 'Listen Without Prejudice' would have sold more in this country. I still am happy with my position here because the music was heard on the radio, and I'm afraid I have to refer you again to the fact that the radio promotion has absolutely nothing to do with CBS UK. I'm quite happy to believe that if they were promoting on radio they would do a good job, but I am just telling you that my personal promotions man did an excellent job and he had nothing to do with CBS UK or Sony UK.
Chancery High Court 1993

Shortly after his case against Sony was dismissed, George Michael gave an interview with David Frost for Carlton TV to talk about his thoughts on the Sony court case.

It wasn't a perfect deal because all the way through, I never signed a new deal. Signing a piece of paper which updates the deal, I mean, every single deal that I have done, every single re-negotiation that I've ever done, whether it be with CBS or Sony, has been an extension of the deal that I signed when I was 18-years-old, which effectively bound me for, I think it was ten albums actually altogether. It was five and an optional five which is effectively the whole of my career, I imagine. I've never been able to sign a piece of paper as a new deal. I've always been trying to update that deal that I did when I was 18, so I've always been held to that part of the deal that I signed when I was 18 years old.

People throw around the figures, these massive figures and massive amounts of money that I was supposedly given by Sony. Now, I will completely agree that they are massive amounts of money, and I am fully aware that I am in a business which pays amazing money, but CBS signed Wham! in 1983. Everything that I have been given by Sony, whether it was in 1984, whether it was in 1988, 1990, they have never been giving me anything above the royalties that I had already earned.

I was paid 11 million pounds. Actually, I didn't realise that I had been paid 11 million pounds, that came out in the court case, but I was paid a huge amount of money – and I know it's a vast amount of money – in 1988, but I was never given anything that CBS, or then, Sony, had already collected from the public. They were always in profit with me. No one ever did me a favour, and said, "Here George, here's 11 million pounds, you know, let's see if we can make it back." They were always working in the black as it were.

You are almost always signing people in a very vulnerable position, and I definitely was in a very vulnerable position. I was at the age of 18, and many bands are signed that young, some are signed a little older, but whenever they're signed, they're desperate. There isn't one other industry that operates on this basis. If I were an author, and I fell out with my company in the way that I have, the worst I would have to endure was the fact that they would have the first option on my next book, so you're talking about two books. It's a ridiculous situation to sign a contract when you're 18 years old, and be held to it for your entire professional career. Why, why, would any court uphold that situation? The judge seems to have found, in my case, that I reaffirmed this contract at the given point of my re-negotiations, but did I really have any choice? The choice that I had was to go along with that length of term, or to do what I've done now, which has been incredibly difficult.

From my point of view, I really, honestly, do not expect the public to have any great sympathy for a man who's very wealthy, you know... I'm in good health, I'm very wealthy, and I have a lot of public support, and I completely accept that. I am not looking for public sympathy. I just don't believe that if you are wealthy... that you are not supposed to fight for your principles.

The trouble is that this business is not like working in an office, or working for any company. If you really fall out with the people who control your professional life, you have a right to walk away. Most people, in whatever situation in life, in whatever job, have the right to say: "If you don't want me any more, if you don't want to work with me any more, if you don't like the way I work, well, sod you. I'm going somewhere else. I may take a smaller wage packet. I may have to work somewhere I don't like as much as this building. I may have to do all kinds of things that I don't want to, but I'm free to do it." That is the right of every individual, and the music industry takes away that right from every artist it signs.

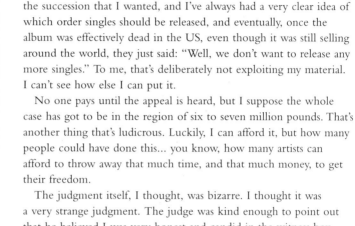

It got to the stage where for the first time in my career, Sony in the US was refusing to release the singles that I wanted in the succession that I wanted, and I've always had a very clear idea of which order singles should be released, and eventually, once the album was effectively dead in the US, even though it was still selling around the world, they just said: "Well, we don't want to release any more singles." To me, that's deliberately not exploiting my material. I can't see how else I can put it.

No one pays until the appeal is heard, but I suppose the whole case has got to be in the region of six to seven million pounds. That's another thing that's ludicrous. Luckily, I can afford it, but how many people could have done this... you know, how many artists can afford to throw away that much time, and that much money, to get their freedom.

The judgment itself, I thought, was bizarre. I thought it was a very strange judgment. The judge was kind enough to point out that he believed I was very honest and candid in the witness box, so I did my best to be truthful and at the same time, he completely accepted everybody on Sony's side. Everybody that appeared in defence of Sony... he completely accepted that they were all telling the truth. Now, if they were all telling the truth about the events that happened between 1990, and the time the writ was served, then, why was I not lying? Somebody was lying.

The ultimate truth is Sony didn't need me to begin with. Sony as a corporation is so massive, and even as a record company, is so massive that they can do without George Michael perfectly easily. The UK company would miss me, the company as a whole would not miss me because it has so many major artists. What they did mean to do with this court case was hold on to their standard contract, and with this judgment they've managed to do that.

If they (Sony) were that reasonable, this would never have got to court in the first place. If they'd been reasonable I could have said: "Look, I don't want to tell the world that this is going on, please let me go. I've been with you for ten years, I've made you hundreds of millions of dollars, and people will believe the deal is over, you know, I've been here this long." They wouldn't accept that. They wouldn't come close to accepting that. I have no real reason to believe that they'll be reasonable before the court of appeal, so, I think, that ultimately, I think it's going to end up in the court of appeal. It's not what I want, but, I think, that's where it's going to be.

I'm trying not to look beyond the possibility of the appeal. I mean, I've lost everything in terms of what I tried to achieve with this action, and I'm an optimist, I've always been an optimist, and it's the only way I can get through to next year, and not crumble under it. I have to believe that this judgment is wrong.

And after the judgment:

I'm determined not to be beaten. This is just the first hurdle.
I am going to battle on.
Daily Mirror 1994

Musicians do not come in regimented shapes and sizes, but are
individuals who evolve together. Sony obviously views this as a great
inconvenience. I am now convinced that, without a total artistic
and personal compromise on my part, the sad deterioration in my
relations with Sony worldwide is irreversible.
Daily Mail 1994

I shall obviously take full legal advice, but the initial view is that
we have very strong grounds for an appeal.
Daily Telegraph 1994

I'm shocked at the judgment. It means that even though I both
created and paid for my work, I will never own it or have any rights
over it. And perhaps most importantly, I have no right to resign.
In fact there is no such thing as resignation of an artist in the music
industry. However, I'm convinced that the English legal system will
not uphold what is effectively professional slavery.
The Sun 1994

I wish it had never gone this far. The whole thing was decided before I got there, it's very sad. It's not the fact that he (Mr Justice Parker) dismissed the case, it's the fact that over six months he didn't consider one word I'd said.

Sunday Express 1994

And the comments of others:

To say that he was not overawed by the formalities of the proceedings may be something of an understatement, but his evidence was certainly none the worse for that. He was refreshingly candid, and I have no doubt at all that in giving his evidence he was doing his best to do so fairly and honestly and to assist me to the best of his recollection and to the best of his knowledge.

Mr Justice Parker, Daily Telegraph 1994

I love George. I love his music. I don't really know what all this court case has been about, but I can't believe I won't be able to buy another George Michael record until the next century. It's heartbreaking.

Eileen Robertson, a fan 1994

I feel very sorry for George. He's a creative artist so he'll want to create. He'll just have to find a different environment to do it in, and I wish him the best of luck.

Ed Bicknell Dire Straits manager 1994

I think the judge has been sensible to throw this out of court.
It would have been better if George had spent more time making
music than being in court. I think he has behaved disgracefully.
George is a star who has a temper tantrum and has been a prima
donna stamping his foot.
Jonathan King 1994

It's all Greek to me.
Mark King, Level 42 1994

Why can't George Michael do what he wants? Why can't he
write a ballet if he wants to?
Prince 1994

Why shouldn't George Michael be able to change the way he
runs his career? If he doesn't want to make videos and tour the way
he once did, then why should he?
Diana Ross 1994

We have great respect for George Michael and his artistry and
look forward to continuing our relationship with him.
Sony Music 1994

It's a crushing blow but he's only lost the first round. George is man
enough to go 15 rounds.
Tony Parsons, biographer 1994

I am sure he will record again one day. But at the moment he
cannot record, sing or release his own work.
Dick Leahy, music publisher & close friend 1994

My manager Clive Banks and I are ecstatic to be free of the
Sony contract. We now have everything George Michael wishes
he could have.
Paul Young (Recently parted company with Sony) 1994

I think he would've got more joy if he'd sued his hairdresser rather
than his record company.
Billy Bragg 1994

If (George) Michael had won, it would have meant no contract
would ever be legal. But anyone worth £80 million and claiming
he's hard done by should look at today's rail strike. I formed my
own company and distributed my music through a major
international company. I retain all the rights. He had that choice
in 1988, but chose to take the cash and the cash offered by Sony
was enormous by 1988 standards.
Peter Waterman 1994

George Michael is an exceptional talent. He is one of the few artists to have successfully crossed from an initial teen audience to mass adult appeal. Similar, indeed, to our own situation. Like Wet Wet Wet, he has had to fight cynicism and negativity from the media, the general public and from his own record label. We totally sympathise with his plight. George has shown magnificent bravery in his attempt to secure release from his Sony record contract. It is a tragedy that he has (so far) failed. Record contracts, despite recent reports to the contrary are still very much biased towards the recording company. Artists have to pay the recording costs and even when recouped they still don't own the copyright. They have to contribute to TV campaigns, tour support costs and quite frankly, just about anything the record companies feel they can get away with.

Not knowing enough of the facts, we do not think it wise to comment on the specifics of the ruling, but the one-sideness of it certainly appears most peculiar. How can Sony have been so right where George and manager were so wrong? We wish George Michael every success in future and the sooner he gets back to doing what he does so well, the better for all of us. We also hope record companies take note of the preparedness of artists to consider artistry before accountancy.

Wet Wet Wet, Q 1994

It would be unjust to Sony if the 1988 agreement were now treated as void. I am satisfied that there is no substance in George Michael's claim of unfair conduct by Sony.

Mr Justice Parker 1994

George on stage at Wembley with Paul Young.

Heroes, Friends & Enemies

Elton John
He's been a musical hero of mine for years. I was desperate to sing backing vocals on an Elton track. But I only plucked up courage to ask by getting drunk at his birthday party. I was scared stiff but he was great about it.

Margaret Thatcher
I think Thatcher has done a lot of damage, but she has given kids new drive. There was a lot of apathy a few years ago, but she has changed all that.
Today 1989

Arthur Scargill
I didn't like Scargill at all. He's awful. I think he's the worst thing the miners could have. He's enjoying the whole thing. That's what's so horrible.
Today 1989

Andrew Ridgeley
Andrew always wanted to be either a footballer or a pop star.
Today 1990

Boy George
Next time I see Boy George, I'll kick him where it hurts.
The Sun 1990

Freddie Mercury
I was very, very sad to hear of Freddie's death. I am still deeply upset by it – it's a tragedy. I had always admired Freddie and his music.

Accountant
My accountant doesn't actually have a firm grip on my creative decisions.
Chancery High Court 1993

The imagery and sense of what Wham! was came from Andrew. When George was younger he wasn't pleased with the way he looked... so he copied Andrew. Eventually he became a pretty good lookalike. So contrary to what people say Wham! was Andrew.
Simon Napier-Bell, former manager. Today - 1990

With Boy George.

Simon Napier-Bell
I never had a very trusting relationship with Simon Napier-Bell.
I remember saying to him on a plane after I'd had a few glasses of
wine: "You know I don't trust you, don't you?"
Daily Mail 1990

(George) Michael should thank the good Lord every morning
when he wakes up to have all that he has... and that'll make two of
us thanking God every morning for all that we have. The tragedy of
fame is when no one shows up and you're singing to the cleaning
lady in some empty joint. Here's a kid who wanted to be a pop star
since he was about seventeen years old. Now that he's a smash
performer and songwriter at 27 he wants to quit doing what tons
of gifted youngsters all over the world would shoot grandma for.
I don't understand a guy who lives in hope of reducing the strain of
his celebrity status.
Frank Sinatra 1990

I really enjoyed making the film with George. I don't pose naked
often, but I was quite happy to do it for this video ('Freedom')
because George made it almost a work of art.
Cindy Crawford, The Sun 1990

With Cindy Crawford.

He has one of the best voices I've ever heard. Technically it's
way ahead of mine. When I first saw George and Andrew Ridgeley
together they reminded me of when Bernie Taupin and I first started
writing songs together. He's also a great songwriter. I'd put him up
there with Paul McCartney.
Elton John

George is one of the most secretive people I know. I am not sure
how he feels most of the time. He is one of those people you have
to push to get anything out of, otherwise he will just carry on
playing "I'm okay, I'm coping".
Shirlie Holliman, close friend

Indiscretion

At the end of the day part of me has to believe that some of the kick was that I might get found out. Well, here I am – I got found out. I don't suppose it will be exciting any more.
News Of The World 1998

I want people to know that I have not been exposed as a gay man in any way that I feel any shame…

I won't even attempt to deny that this is the first time it has happened. I have put myself in this position before. And I can only apologise and try to fathom why I did it. Try to understand my own sexuality for better.
News Of The World 1998

I'd like to put to rest some misconceptions – full stop. The greatest misconception of this week is that I've had the most hellish time. Well, it has not been a good time but it has not been the worst time of my life, by any means. It has been humiliating, embarrassing and funny to some degree. I have been reading reports I was led away crying and, you know, devastated and this and that. The truth was I was led away quite angry. Well angry at myself and the situation. I did not, believe me, try to convince the arresting officer that I was looking for my lottery ticket when he arrested me.
News Of The World 1998

I've been living in a circus, you know. In the middle of a circus with helicopters flying around my house. Literally hundreds of people outside the house waiting day and night for something. I don't know what exactly. Reconstruction? I don't know what they wanted.
News Of The World 1998

I feel stupid and I feel reckless and weak for having allowed my sexuality to be exposed in this way. But I don't feel any shame whatsoever. And neither do I think I should.
News Of The World 1998

I do want to tell my fans, who I feel I have embarrassed to some degree, as I have embarrassed myself, that I am OK. This is not going to finish me off. This is really nothing compared to the bereavements and the legal stuff I have had to deal with.
Mail On Sunday 1998

George's St. Tropez home.

Important Note: Please go before you come as all conveniences will be locked to protect the Host.

Party invite to his 35th birthday 1998

If it hadn't happened that day, it was going to happen very soon. But going through two bereavements gives unrivalled perspective. The first day I was freaked out because I'd literally just got out of depression. I thought, 'Somebody is trying to finish me off here, I cannot be this unlucky, when do I get a fucking break?' I couldn't believe it had happened.

Q 1998

It's disgusting, completely disgusting. The Beverly Hills police sold this ridiculous arrest report to *The Sun*, with all its fucking lies.

Q 1998

I did it because I couldn't resist a free lunch. Is there an element in me that thought, 'Fuck it, if I get caught I get caught?' Yes of course. I've actually had people ask me if I planned it: 'Let's face it George, you couldn't get arrested in America…'

Q 1998

The truth is that there were three people. Two undercover cops and a randy pop star who'd had a couple of drinks at lunch. I didn't come… Um, I don't mean 'come'. I didn't go anywhere near the guy. He started playing 'I'll show you mine, you show me yours. And when you show me yours, I'll nick you'. That's what happened. I was angry.

He was quite tasty. They don't sent Karl Malden in there, we're not talking Columbo with his dick out. They only need a quick flash to arrest, so he was off quickly. I stood there thinking, 'Hmmm that was weird.' I assumed he was unimpressed.

As far as I was concerned, I wasn't followed into that toilet by someone shifty. I responded to something that I shouldn't have, but I don't think anyone in a thousand years looks at a man waving him penis at them and thinks, 'Oh he's got to be a cop'… if there's nobody around except for you and someone who wants a bit of fun? Why'd I think I'd be unlucky enough for that to happen? That's what people do! If men pick each other up, they show each other their dicks! That's how it works! They don't usually get nicked! Why should I think he's a cop?

I took that risk. There are many times I wouldn't have. In the arrest report, the guy said he was simulating urination. Excuse me? If you try that at home you'll get wee all over the shop. If you see a man playing with his penis in front of you, you don't think it's a cop. I don't understand why it's

more legal for a cop to go into a toilet and wave his dick at people than it is for someone who wants to do it. Only they get paid for it. What goes on the CV? Professional wanker? Oh, that's my title at the moment. I don't know. It's all beyond me.

In 1998 I didn't believe people went to that degree to induce crime. That's not what American tax payers think their money is being spent on. Everyone knows that people come on to each other in those places. I was stupid, I shouldn't have done it, it's against the law, but what happened that afternoon was totally unfair. I apologise to people if it offends them, but it's not like anything outrageous happened. If it does offend them they're not likely to be fans, so why would I worry? I'm not interested in the views of homophobes or people's perceptions of me outside those who like my music. I have nothing to apologise for. I could not believe they had fucking done this to me. I was totally totally stitched up.
Q 1998

Lawyers tell me everybody knows this is going on, everyone of these reports looks the same. They make up bullshit arrest reports so people are terrified to fight them in court. This shit has been going on year in, year out. It's easy convictions. Was I prepared to stand in court and call the man who wrote the arrest report a liar? My word against a policeman's? If I were not a celebrity I'd have done it and claimed entrapment, but not on fucking worldwide television. It's not an option for a celebrity.
Q 1998

My favourite joke followed the false report which said two police officers walked in as I was having a good old knuckle shuffle, didn't stop and apparently I went, 'Hello guys, here it is. What's the difference between George Michael and a microwave? A microwave stops when you open the door.'
Q 1998

I've had the privilege of being seen in my worst possible incarnation and people being alright with it. If you've been the soundtrack to somebody's life, they'll be a little more forgiving. I responded with honesty. People said, 'Fuck it, we don't care.'
Q 1998

I'll never get arrested again. Look you've got to understand it never should have happened. It didn't happen by accident. Am I going to put myself in a public situation like that again? Of course not. Are they going to try and humiliate me again? Very possibly.

This has been something which I've ended up writing a couple of decent songs about. As long a I get a smash Number 1, I won't care. I'm being flippant, but only because I've made a smash record and I don't need extra publicity. As long as people buy my records, it makes what I don't like easier to stomach. It's a means to the end of having people hear my music. If my record's all over the radio and part of the interest is based on that scandal, then fucked up though that is, fine. So be it.

I don't want it to stay around, but I'm not going to kick it out the door. I have no problem with it lodging in people's memory, it makes no difference to me.
Q 1998

If he would think of reconsidering his position, I would work here at Project Angel Food for as many hours as he sees fit, not just the 80 hours that I've been given.

Judge Rubin, I remain at your mercy. But whatever you think of me or my behaviour, please, please do not let this unusual opportunity for good go to waste… (I am) fully aware that, in all likelihood, I have prompted (the judge's) sudden change of heart by my own actions.
1998, after the 'Outside' video prompted a stiffening of his community service sentence

Megastars are people who've had luck and managed risk successfully. Part of the thrill could have been the risk of being found out and losing everything. George has achieved huge success and access to power. He could almost be saying, 'Could I survive breaking the ultimate taboo?' It's like self-validation. If his reputation survives this he knows he's a true megastar because only a megastar could.
Dr Patrick McGhee, psychologist, Sun 1998

Coming Out

I think people really seem to like to talk about it. I totally understand the debate, I have a real strong theory as to why people are so obsessed with one another's sexuality. And because I have that belief about it, I see absolutely no, I feel no obligation to join the debate, put it that way. I think it's a perfectly understandable question, I have no problem with everyone thinking I am gay, or some people thinking I'm gay, some people thinking that I'm straight or whatever. I think it's totally, totally, irrelevant to my life, that everyone else is talking about my sexuality because all the people that I know and care about are perfectly clued in, I mean everybody knows who I am.

So for the sake of people that I never speak to I really don't feel any desire to define myself. I'll tell you what I really believe. I believe that we all sit, look at each other and we all, I think every human being constantly questions themselves. Questions their own position, whether it be their race, their religion, their sexuality, their looks, you know, we all question ourselves, and use other people to define ourselves.

I think that one of the things that is so difficult in the modern world to actually accept, is that sexuality is a really, really blurry thing. I know lots and lots of people who I thought were of one sexual persuasion, but they turned out to either be the other, or sometimes to be the other, so that, whatever. All I know, is that I have never, never, regarded my sexuality as a moral question, of any description. Or anyone's sexuality as a moral question, other than when it is some kind of twisted sexuality that involves people that do not give their consent, you know. But I, personally, have never thought that would be wrong, that would be right, that's what I should do. I think, most people do regard their sexuality as a moral question, and I think that they look to one another to reinforce their ideas of themselves.

In other words, if somebody looks at me, and says, 'I think he's gay', and then next week, I make a statement saying, 'I am gay', right, that guy feels a little bit more secure in the fact that he knew that that was my sexuality. Whether he was right or wrong, do you know whether I'm telling the truth or not, people use it as the…it's the typical old thing, the queen that stands in the gay club, or standing in the straight club, pointing out all the people that he thinks are gay.

Radio 1 1997

They're saying, 'I know what a gay person looks like, I know what a straight person looks like'. Therefore, in most people it's in an effort to prove that they are straight themselves. Because, obviously, being straight is the socially acceptable and the most common, human form of sexuality.

George with Elton John.

But most people…have some questions at some point in their life, and even if they are very young when they have those questions or whatever, they scare the shit out of them… And, one of the ways that they reinforce their own idea of their own sexuality, whatever it may be, is to tell themselves that they can spot it in other people, and that they can spot people who are of different sexual persuasions, and that's why you get a huge debate about somebody like me.

You've got all these guys for instance, maybe their girlfriend likes me or whatever, and they're like, 'Oh, he's a fairy, its obvious to me', now, if they were wrong, if they were proved to be wrong, that would be unsettling for them. If they were proved to be right, that would be comforting for them. That's what I mean. It is literally as simple as that. I'm right, I know who he is, because I know who I am. I know his sexuality because I know mine.

Now, I have got absolutely no desire, to be that for people. Do you know what I mean? I've got no desire to stand up and define myself to a whole bunch of people, and say 'yes, I was right', or 'no, I was wrong', or 'no, you were wrong'. Do you know what I mean?'

Radio 1 1997

'I define my sexuality in terms of the people that I love and my life right now is very happy living in a gay relationship. I'm very happy with that; I don't look to the future and think I might change my sexuality because I'm hoping that my relationship is the one that is going to last me for the rest of my life.

I mean I could've tried to put any number of angles on this tonight, but ultimately at the end of the day I'm not ashamed, I'm just pissed with myself for having been so stupid. And I'm perfectly prepared to believe that as long as I am truthful to myself and truthful to the people who are out there with my music then I have nothing to fear.

CNN 1998

I have no problem with people knowing that I'm in a relationship with a man right now. I have not been in a relationship with a woman for almost ten years.

News Of The World 1998

I do want people to know that the songs I wrote when I was with women were really about women. The songs I have written since were fairly obviously about men. So I think in terms of my work, I have never been reticent in terms of defining my sexuality.

News Of The World 1998

I spent the first half of my career accused of being gay when I hadn't had anything like a gay relationship. I was 27 before that happened to me. So I spent my years growing up being told what my sexuality was really, you know, which was kind of confusing.

Then, by the time I'd kind of worked out what it was, I had stopped having relationships with women. I was just so indignant at the way I had been treated till then, I just thought 'I will hold on to this. I don't think they need to know. I don't think I have to tell them'. But this is as good a time as any.

News Of The World 1998

If every star in the world came out, it wouldn't make any difference to the gay community. Someone like me who sits there with the big neon question mark above my head and openly invites those questions is, therefore, a fascination. I think everything about me has always been ambiguous.

Big Issue 1998

For someone who'd had as much nookie as me, I was terribly under-developed emotionally. I knew what it was all about but I had no idea what falling in love was. Sexuality's not about who you can get it up for; it's about who you can get up for and fall in love with.

Q 1998

If I was not someone who knew about women, I wouldn't have the audience I have. People don't want to hear that, but it's the truth. I spent the first part of my adulthood not being in love, fucking around, fucking men, fucking women, thinking I was bisexual. I had no proof of anything deeper. It could have gone on indefinitely if I'd kept working and taking public admiration as replacement for the real thing.

Q 1998

Running naked up and down Oxford Street singing 'I Am What I Am' would have been a more dignified way to come out.

Q 1998

My favourite, favourite motto is a Jean Cocteau quote: never state what you can imply. It's got me into a lot of trouble recently.

Q 1998

I've been openly gay with everyone in my life for eight or nine years now. The paparazzi don't want to hear that I'm perfectly fine with my sexuality

George with hairdresser Nicky Clark and Andreas Georgiou.

With k.d. lang.

or that I have a fantastic relationship. They want to hear the hard luck story of the poor closeted pop star.

That's not what people are going to get because it isn't like that. If it were, I would have been destroyed by my arrest. That's what they wanted. Also, as far as I was concerned, I'd come out in my work. People might have looked at my not being out with the tabloids as dishonest. I couldn't think of anything more honest.

Anyway, if you don't want people to think you're gay, you don't grow a moustache that makes you look like you've failed a Village People audition. Who was there left to say I Am Gay to, other than to people who it didn't matter to.

Q 1998

George with partner Kenny Goss.

I've had to put up with Boy George for 12 years doing the whole closeted thing. I've always been nice to him, talked to him about my boyfriends and he still has a go. Leave it out. What is his problem? I'm hardly going to take spiritual or career guidance from him.

Q 1998

It's a real embarrassment for me to go to the toilet these days. I have to make sure there's no one in the vicinity in case I scare them out.

Q 1998

His Men

After Anselmo died I went through bereavement counselling which helped a lot. I'm not naturally depressive. I mean I've suffered from depression in depressive circumstances but I don't have a tendency towards it. I'm not very good at wallowing. If I'm going to feel bad I distract myself. (Two tracks on Older, 'Jesus To A Child' and 'You Have Been Loved', are about his friend's death.)

It was the most enlightening experience I've ever had. The minute someone you really love is irretrievably lost you understand life in a different way. Your perspective changes. You understand how short life is, how incredibly painful it can be. But once you've seen the worst of things then you can see the best of things.

So that experience was very painful at the time but very positive in its outcome. It was a terrible shock. The grief is always there and sometimes it comes back. You feel it every bit as painfully as if it were yesterday and other times you think of the person and how fantastic the experience of knowing them was.

The really puzzling question that it leaves you with is 'What's more important – to have a long and healthy life or to enjoy every day as it happens?' I've always obsessively invested in the future. But now I wonder if I should spend so much time worrying about it – there might not be a future.

Big Issue 1998

With Versace and Elton John.

(Anselmo) took away that slightly puritanical, Victorian aspect of my upbringing. (the relationship) was the most enlightening experience I have ever had.

Telegraph 1998

He was the love of my life. He was the one who taught me that I was gay. Anselmo lived life on the edge – and he infected me with that excitement.

National Enquirer 1998

For the first time I got together with someone I thought loved me. I actually felt that I loved him.

Q 1998

Being unfaithful to Kenny (Goss, partner) was the crime. That's the crime as far as I'm concerned. I'm not saying I have an open situation with my boyfriend but he knows how I am. He knows that I'm generally over-sexed. He's been very, very good. We love each other and he understands that it was a stupid mistake and he's forgiven me… I hope.

Daily Star 1998

More Music
Older

I know fans will be disappointed that I've given up the ghost and I'm not sprinting from one end of the stage to the other any, but I just can't do it. I've got a bad back. That's what 'Older' really means. My discs are going. 'He's gone from gold discs to slipped discs.'
Radio 1 1996

There's a song on the album called 'It Doesn't Really Matter', which is one of my favourite songs on there. But that has literally got one of those little old…do you remember those Dr Rhythm boxes? The first rhythm synthesisers, and it's just got a little Dr Rhythm thing going on, bass guitar, and me playing a few piano chords, I think…I did play it all. It's one of the simplest things I've ever recorded, and it's right in the middle of the album, and the rest of it is quite heavily produced. I love that, I really love that, but, a remarkable number of people don't notice the song.
Radio 1 1997

Well, luckily, a couple of my closest friends take great pleasure in putting me down, so I've got people who would tell me, absolutely, this is a pile of shit, don't put this out. But, in all honesty, I'm very, very self-critical, and I throw away an awful lot of stuff. I'm not a Prince type that can lay hundreds and hundreds of tracks down and think that because they're me, that they must be good. I throw an awful lot of material away because I just know it's not up to scratch. It's quite often material that other people like.
Radio 1 1997

I was still grieving very heavily. I was trying to write but when I'm not listening to music I dry up and I was too fragile to listen to anything that would take me anywhere depressing. At the end of 1994, 18 months later, I wrote 'Jesus To A Child' and I was back. Phew.
Q 1998

If I'd been trying to come into this business now, I'd have given up. My attitude then – You fuckers don't know anything – wouldn't get me anywhere. I've realised that if you're looking for long-term vision or respect from record companies, forget it. One minute I was the fastest-selling album on Virgin ever (with 'Older'), two months later the Spice Girls arrive…
Q 1998

Ladies and Gentlemen... Greatest Hits

I want the album to do well. It clearly shows the two sides of my appeal: fuck-off pop records people can't resist and songs that make people feel. And (Sony are) putting it out at a reasonable price, which I'm pleased about.
Q 1998

... the only thing I can think of in the near future is... getting out of my Sony contract, by promising three new tracks for the greatest hits album... Well... I won't be doing them for Sony, you see, I'll be doing them for my greatest hits album, and – having waited for 14 or 13 years to do one – I want it to be a great album. I want it to have the best of my stuff on it, and I want it to have three killer new tracks on it. That's for me, that's not for Sony. So I will, it's just the time frame I actually have to, contractually, deliver these things by a certain date. That's the difficult bit. In terms of actually doing the three new tracks, I'm doing them for me, not for them.
Radio 1 1997

Mary is thrilled with the track as far as I know, and it's one of the best performances she's ever given. So I think she's really pissed off that it's not going to be out here in the States. I'm sure it will be a big hit in the rest of the world, which (is great, because) actually she's not recognised as much as she should be outside of America. It's the reverse situation to mine. I think it will really break her open in the rest of the world. It's a real shame that it's not going to be out over here.
1998, when Mary J Blige's duet on 'As' was dropped from the US album for record-company reasons

His record label, Aegean

Aegean is based around song, that's our focus. We're not about pop music, but quality material. Apart from being the owner, George is the A&R man and we don't sign anybody or do anything musically without consulting him. We're lucky to have one of the best A&R men in the country.
Andreas Georgiou, President Aegean, Music Week 1997

Toby (Bourke) is actually the first person that I was introduced to...and in fact this song 'Waltz Away Dreaming' is actually an adaptation of the original demo I heard, and the B-side is actually completely a demo. It's just a guitar and Toby singing and he just is the most fantastic writer, fantastic singer.

The reason for him coming first was simply that I was listening to the

original demo a couple of nights after my mum died and it just seemed like a perfect...I knew that if I adapted the lyrics a little and added my own verses, that it would just be, could be a wonderful song. Just in terms of paying tribute to my mum you know, and the way it should be heard really is if you listen to it basically Toby's voice represents my father's voice, and I represent myself talking to my father, and I'm very proud of it...

I've always said it's the first release partly in tribute to my mother, and secondly, the fact that I'm involved in it obviously is a nice way to start out. But...this has not actually been a particularly easy record on radio which I knew it wouldn't be. You know, if I wasn't on it the chances are because of its tempo, and because of the style of it, that it wouldn't really get listened to. But regardless of that, I knew it would have to be the first thing...simply because...it's I think a very high quality song and performance from Toby and I wanted to show people from the out that quality is what the label's going to be about.

GWR FM 1997

... having my own record company is really about trying, having a corner in the industry where artist know they can come if they want kind of respect and freedom to do what they want and basically its about 50/50, you know its all about...doing the best work and them having doing their best work and being free to leave if they are not happy. The success of the label is really about my decisions, my choices. Who I think has got the talent to do this, so really if I fail miserably it will all be down to me. I am aware of that.

Capital Radio 1997

Addictions

I smoke incessantly when I'm with people who smoke incessantly. I smoke because I started, when I had… real kinds of reasons, but I had a real low point about five years ago, and I smoked. I started to smoke grass to relieve stress and whatever, and because I didn't want to be on any kind of sedatives or…

Smoking is the most stupid thing I've ever done, it's the worst thing for my health. It's completely out of control but, somehow, I think I've got control over it, because I don't roll my own joints, which means I can't go home with a bag of grass and sit and get stoned out of my head. I have to have someone smoking with me.

Radio 1 1997

To tell you the truth, the reason that I stopped drinking red wine… was that I was informed that it was the absolute worst kind of alcohol for a singer. Red wine makes your sinuses swell and stuff like that, so I stopped. But, of course, when I started smoking cigarettes there wasn't much point in changing over, I should have stuck to the red I think.

Radio 1 1997

I started smoking grass because it was either that or some kind of medication which I didn't want to take. This time last year I was a complete and utter pothead. I know it's lunacy but the whole truth is that the grass really helped me with the lyrics.

I'd know there was something I really wanted to say but I wouldn't know how to say it. So I'd have a few drags and stand behind the mike and in a few minutes I'd be there. It's bad because I don't want to smoke but I can't see myself giving up grass as a writer.

Big Issue 1998

It's the only way to work. I light a joint at the end of 'Spinning The Wheel'. You hear a lighter, then you hear it burning and me going (sucking noise), then, Pahhh, and the next track starts. I don't want to sing about drugs though, how boring.

The media and music industry have been incredibly irresponsible in making drugs essential to youth culture. Look at how Happy Mondays were written about and Oasis are written about. It's fine if you've got a habit and the money to do it, but it does nobody favours to make out it's an integral part of making music. I made lots of music before I took drugs that was just as good.

Q 1998

I'm a grass and occasional ecstasy man. I wish I'd never taken ecstasy because I wouldn't know what I was missing. I've never thrown up on it, never had a headache. I'm very good with drugs, but I find cocaine offensive – it's the new alcohol.

It's fashionable to take heroin again, so you've got perfectly intelligent people doing the most stupid thing. It's looked at as heroic. It doesn't matter how horrific *Trainspotting* is if you give it the coolest soundtrack of the last five years. I didn't take drugs until my fucking bones had stopped growing. At least I was the shape of an adult.

Q 1998